How I Didn't Become a
Become a
BEATLE

How I Didn't Become a
BEATLE

BRIAN HUDSON

THE HISTORY PRESS

First published in the United Kingdom in 2008 by
The History Press
Cirencester Road · Chalford · Stroud · Gloucestershire · GL6 8PE

British Library Cataloguing in Publication Data
A catalogue record for this book is available from the British Library.

ISBN 978-0-7509-4955-2

Typeset in 11.5/13.5 Galliard
Typesetting and origination by
The History Press.
Printed and bound in England.

This book is dedicated to
all the people who have been touched by Liverpool.

———◆———

' . . . the sensation of life, exquisite when it is not painful.'

Rebecca West, *I Believe*, 1940

'Life is what happens to you while you're busy making other plans.'

John Lennon, *Beautiful Boy*, 1980

CONTENTS

ABOUT THE AUTHOR

Yorkshire-born Brian Hudson now lives in Brisbane, Australia, having migrated from Jamaica with his family in 1985. He and his wife, Anne both teach at the Queensland University of Technology where Brian is an Adjunct Professor in the School of Urban Development.

AUTHOR'S NOTE & ACKNOWLEDGEMENTS

I was a young drummer on the Liverpool Scene in the late 1950s and early '60s. One of the bands in which I played regularly is often mentioned in books about The Beatles, whose early story includes their search for a suitable drummer. I was not invited to join them; I never applied. Ringo got the job.

One day, he and his fellow Beatles drove past me in a limousine as I watched from the top deck of a Liverpool Corporation bus. They went on to unprecedented fame and fortune in the world of popular music. I didn't. But I, too, was soon to begin a career that took me all over the world and would enrich me with undreamed of experiences. The following chapters record some of them. The main characters in my story are the city of Liverpool and the people who lived there at the time when the Mersey Sound burst upon the world.

This account relies largely on my memory, but letters and postcards that I sent home during my student days, correspondence preserved by my late parents, have helped me. Scant and often cryptic entries in old diaries and notebooks also provided a useful source. I have tried to be as accurate as possible but memory does play tricks; and, of course, I cannot recall exactly the spoken words I uttered and heard all those years ago. In a few cases I have changed personal names where I thought it preferable to hide identity. Phil Morris, Bill Hart, Tony Teale, Gus Craik, Ron Lloyd, Keith Allcock, John Rotherham, Hugh Potter, John Chambers, Jim Trimmer, John Wilson, Dave Twiss, John Haylett, Norma Herdson and the late John Barnes are among those to whom I am indebted for kindly reading and commenting on earlier versions of the manuscript or searching their memories to help me. My wife, Anne, also helped me very much in this way and I am grateful for her unfailing support and encouragement at all times.

For editorial help and advice, I owe a debt of gratitude to Neil Marr whom I met, very appropriately, through Fred Burnett's wonderful Jazznorthwest website. My thanks, too, to Michelle Tilling and Simon Fletcher of Sutton Publishing for being receptive to my ideas and smoothing the path to publication.

Except where indicated, all the photographs and drawings are from the author's collection. I am grateful to Simpson's Photographic Services, Liverpool; Bill Harry, editor of *Mersey Beat*; John Haylett, editor of the *Morning Star*; and Liverpool City Council for permission to use illustrative material in their copyright ownership.

Brian Hudson
Brisbane, Australia,
March 2008

CHAPTER ONE

LIVERPOOL DRUMMER

The narrow entrance and the grimy steps down into that hot, smelly, crowded, noisy cellar might have been compared to the gates of Hell. To me, a nineteen-year-old student newly arrived in Liverpool, it was more like discovering Heaven.

The Cavern had opened only a few months earlier and that night in 1957 its resident group, the Merseysippi Jazz Band, was playing. This was how I had always imagined a real jazz club to be; a dingy cellar filled with devotees listening to inspired musicians. Until then, my experience of jazz had been confined to radio broadcasts, a few records – 78s, EPs and LPs – some films like *The Glenn Miller Story* and *The Benny Goodman Story*, and one jazz concert – Louis Armstrong and the Allstars at London's Empress Hall in 1956. That vast, impersonal venue was better known for boxing matches and the revolving stage on which the band played, caused the sound to come and go.

Here at The Cavern, with local musicians inspired by Louis, the atmosphere was just right; the band and the audience tightly enclosed in the basement of a converted warehouse. In company with fellow enthusiasts from Liverpool University, I descended into that secular crypt which was soon to become sacred as one of the most famous music venues in the world.

What brought me to Liverpool was a bright working-class grammar schoolboy's desire for a university education and all the imagined privileges it would provide. This and the urge to return to the north of England where I was born. I had spent most of my childhood and teenage life in the genteel Kentish suburbs of London, but I retained a strong attachment to my native North Country with its moors, dales, rugged coast and grim industrial towns.

I was to learn that Liverpool, at the mouth of the River Mersey, was a very different kind of North, very different even from the county of Lancashire, of which it was, at least geographically, a part. Set near the centre of the British Isles, Liverpool has felt the influence of all the countries around it. England, Wales, Scotland, Ireland and the Isle of

The author on drums in the Liverpool University Jazz Band playing in the Gilmour Hall on Friday 13 March 1959. (Reproduced with the permission of Simpson's Photographic Services, Liverpool)

Man were in the melting pot with the world beyond linked by centuries of trade and shipping.

I recall an occasion in a Chinese restaurant where the patrons were the usual Liverpool multi-racial mix, with skin colour ranging from white to black and someone among them was speaking Welsh Gaelic. On a clear day the hills of Wales can be seen from Liverpool and boats and planes maintain close links with Ireland and the Isle of Man. Scotland lies a couple of hours' drive to the north.

So Liverpool – Merseyside – evolved its own distinctive speech, Scouse, a linguistic form of English that became familiar all over the world in the 1960s when The Beatles happened. There was quite a lot of Scouse, with various levels of refinement, at Liverpool University, but accents from all over Britain and beyond were to be heard there. Mine, I suppose, was a kind of slightly northern-tinged south-east London English. Despite the years of life and schooling in the South, my vowels hinted at northern origins. My pronunciation of 'dance' rhymed with the first syllable of 'Kansas', rather than sounding like 'dahnce', the southern way.

For me, university meant the beginning of life as an independent man. I had won a State Scholarship and, while my parents still contributed a little to my keep, I was no longer dependent on them. For the first time, home was not where my parents lived.

The shock of lifestyle change was softened by my first Liverpool lodgings in a family home in Huyton, a suburb similar in many ways to that which I had just left. Encouraged by fellow students who had found rooms near the city centre a short walk from the university, I soon exchanged the familiar world of semi-detached suburbia for a very different life in the decayed terraces and squares of Liverpool 7 and 8.

One of the reasons for this change of residence was my purchase of a second-hand set of drums, which I found through the small ads of the *Liverpool Echo*. It cost me £20 – two weeks' wages for a Liverpool dockworker at the time. I later forked out as much again on expanding and improving my drum kit, spending on it most of what I earned by playing at paid gigs. Cheap and basic, this crudely made 'Broadway' drum set opened up possibilities about which I had long dreamt – and my dream was to be a jazz drummer.

The acquisition also raised a couple of problems. Not only did it threaten the peace of the household, but the relatively long bus ride from Huyton to the city was inconvenient with drum accompaniment. On one occasion, this problem drew witty comment from a bus conductor who was watching me trying to stuff my bass drum, which lacked a cover, and the case containing the rest of the kit into the luggage space under the stair of the double-decker. 'Is dat yer drum?' he asked as I struggled with my burden. 'Yes', I answered, puzzled by the unexpected question. 'Then beat it!' he responded. The bus conductor was 'just 'avin' a bit of a laff' at my expense, his way of welcoming me aboard.

It was the inspiration of the Liverpool University Jazz Band that had persuaded me to blow a huge hole in my very limited funds on a set of drums. I particularly remember relaxing in the Students' Union Library and listening to the Armstrong-influenced trumpet of medical student, John Higham, downstairs in the Gilmour Hall. He was playing *Keeping Out of Mischief Now*. The band he led had earned a proud reputation on the local music scene and in university jazz circles around the country. Among its most outstanding members was bass player Hughie Potter, named best individual musician at the annual Inter-University Jazz Federation band competition in 1957 and 1958. Years later, in 1970, John, by then well established in medical practice, joined the Merseysippi Jazz Band. How I wanted to play with musicians like that.

How I wished I had the ability! My musical education was minimal. An uncle in Yorkshire had introduced me to the rudiments of drumming and my short stint as a trainee drummer with a silver band in Orpington, Kent, had done a little to improve my skill, but I never really mastered the arts of *paradiddle* and *mummy daddy*. Fortunately, I had an ear for music of all kinds, from British folk music and Negro spirituals to popular classics – Handel's *Water Music*, Bach's *Sheep May Safely Graze*, Mendelssohn's *Hebrides Overture*, and Ravel's *Bolero*. Now jazz had become a passion. I had joined the university's jazz society, Rhythm Club, and was desperate to play in a band.

Opportunity came when graduation began to take its toll on Liverpool University musicians, leaving vacancies that younger students were keen to fill. I heard that a new university band was being formed and that it needed a drummer. My informant was a woman who was a year ahead of me in the geography course in which I was enrolled. She worked sometimes at a coffee bar, The Pack of Cards, near the Students' Union, and was aware of what was happening there. She was also familiar with the local jazz scene. One day in the Students' Union she introduced me to a group of young musicians who were forming a new band and they invited me to fill the drumming spot.

They were a mixed lot, including students from various backgrounds. Over time there were personnel changes and among the academic and professional disciplines represented in the band at some time or other were medicine, engineering, veterinary science, dentistry, English, psychology and biochemistry. I was the only geographer in the group

Liverpool University Panto Day, Pier Head, 1958. Phil Morris is playing trumpet, Keith Allcock is on clarinet and his girlfriend Rita Kilgallon (now Keith's wife) is the guitarist. The author is the drummer. (Author's Collection)

and later, as a postgraduate, the only Civic Design student. Liverpool University's School of Architecture had its own jazz band and some other students played in local bands. Except for myself and a Shropshire lad, all the original players were from Merseyside or neighbouring parts of Lancashire and Cheshire. Standards of musical skill varied but several of the jazz musicians had classical training to a high level. An engineering student who joined us later was a Licentiate of the London College of Music. He, like some others in Rhythm Club, was competent on more than one instrument. We practised together in the Union, playing what was generally described as traditional jazz, although there were among us those who had learned to appreciate modern jazz, including bebop. The late Charlie Parker was my jazz idol and the Modern Jazz Quartet was my favourite combo at that time. We recognised that we were unable to play complex music of that standard and wisely stuck to 'trad', only later progressing into mainstream and even beyond.

Liverpool University Panto Day, 1959. Rhythm Club musicians brave the wet weather on the steps of St George's Hall. Again, the author is the drummer. (Author's Collection)

The original group included trumpet, trombone, clarinet, piano, banjo or guitar, and me on drums. We didn't have a bass player to begin with but over the next few years several different students filled that role. During my time at Liverpool, the core group of musicians expanded and contracted. It assumed various forms, ranging from a trio and a Shearing style quintet, complete with vibraphone, to an eleven-piece band that included a full reed section and two French horns.

It was during one of our early practice sessions in the Union that a young woman invited us to play at a function which was to be our band's first gig. I felt elated. It was to be my public debut as a jazz drummer. We were even going to be paid. I was a professional musician at last! Over the next few years, my modest earnings from drumming were spent on improvements to my original drum kit, but I never possessed a good set. Delighted at this opportunity to perform to an audience, we readily accepted the invitation. The occasion was a dance for student teachers and their guests at Barkhill, a women's college in

MANCHESTER UNIVERSITY

ARTS FESTIVAL

JAZZ
BAND
BALL

IN THE UNIVERSITY UNION

3/6

28 November

7-30   11-45

Manchester University Arts Festival Jazz Band Ball ticket.

the suburb of Aigburth. How we got there I don't recall. Very few students had cars in those days. To get to our gigs, we usually stuffed ourselves and our instruments into a small, borrowed van. Sometimes we had to travel considerable distances in this way with scarcely enough room for the driver. Bad weather could make travelling even more difficult. On some trips to Manchester we drove through fog so dense that visibility was down to a couple of yards.

I was later to be reminded of those days early in the twenty-first century, by which time I was a grandfather living in Brisbane, Australia. After listening to a group with the intriguing name of The View from Madeleine's Couch and chatting with the musicians afterwards at a club in the city's Fortitude Valley, I was invited to join them for drinks when they went home. It felt just like old times when a group of us piled into the van with the instruments, including vibraphone and conga drum, with me sitting on the floor at the back of the vehicle together with a visiting American sailor who'd sat in on flute during the band's second set.

Unlike the club performance that night in Brisbane, the Liverpool college dance all those years ago was quite a formal affair with at least some of the dancers in evening dress. Despite our inexperience as a group, we felt confident as we set up on the small stage. We had not prepared a programme but, like true jazzmen, we had in our heads many standard tunes, a legacy we shared as jazz aficionados. We began with a lively number and to our delight, the audience started to dance. Some of the elegantly dressed young couples jived enthusiastically to our music and it felt great to be the drummer, driving the band along and exerting such a powerful influence on the audience.

My newfound musician friends seemed pleasantly surprised at my drumming, one complimenting me by saying that I was 'a natural'. That boosted my confidence and I offered to sing a song I had learned from a Louis Armstrong record but which I had never before sung in public: *Mack the Knife*. After some hesitation, the band began to play the well-known tune and at the appropriate time the leader, no doubt feeling somewhat apprehensive, turned to me for my unrehearsed vocal contribution. Overcoming my nervousness and continuing to beat out the rhythm, I began to sing into the microphone that had been placed beside me. What I did was an imitation of Louis Armstrong's famous vocal performance and my attempt to reproduce that much-loved gravelly voice and exquisite timing was well received by band and audience alike. I basked in the enthusiastic applause I received and the story of my impromptu performance was spread by a student friend who had been in the audience. This gave me quite a reputation for hidden talent and *Mack the Knife* has remained a party piece of mine ever since.

Decades after my public debut as a jazz drummer and singer, I celebrated my sixtieth birthday with family and friends at the Brisbane Jazz Club in Australia. I had issued strict instructions that no one should request the band to play the traditional *Happy Birthday* song, a piece that offends me greatly by its lack of melody and utter banality, as well as the tuneless way in which it is usually sung. Despite my wish, someone did approach the pianist leader of the trad band playing that night and requested the detested song. To avoid being made unhappy by *Happy Birthday*, I offered to sing something myself instead – *Mack the Knife*.

While admitting that he and his fellow musicians knew and could play the song, the man at the piano showed some hesitation about letting a white haired, drink-merry stranger perform with him onstage. Nevertheless, with the support of the part of the audience that comprised my party guests, I was given access to the microphone and the band started to play. As I swung into the song, I sensed in the band

and the audience a feeling of relief that my performance was much better than they expected. There was even a surprised appreciation. My Satchmoesque rendition of the popular song was received with loud applause that encouraged me to demonstrate yet another of my 'hidden talents', a skill originally taught to me as a child by my drummer uncle in Yorkshire. Though I no longer played drums, I was still a maestro on the spoons and I dazzled my Brisbane audience with a virtuoso display of rhythmic cutlery in a way rarely, if ever, before witnessed in a jazz performance.

After that first public performance in Liverpool, band practices and gigs became a regular part of my university life. Most weeks there was a dance at the Students' Union, sometimes two, and our group usually played as support band. On these occasions there was often a nationally famous British jazz band, such as Alex Welsh or Mick Mulligan. Invariably, there were one or two other supporting groups, usually including a top local band together with the university band. The principal band played in the Union's large Stanley Hall, while the university band spent most of its time in the smaller Gilmour Hall. The latter was preferred by some couples who wished to smooch around the dance floor away from the wildly jiving dancers in the larger hall. The university band often took to the Stanley Hall stage while the main band enjoyed a break. There were even times when a third dance hall was used, the students' cafeteria upstairs being temporarily converted for the purpose. It was there that I first met and sat in with the Architects' Jazz Band, briefly taking the place of its exuberant drummer, Seamus McGonagle, an Irishman.

The most formal occasion at which the Rhythm Club Band played was the Science Faculty Ball on Friday, 13 March 1959. The Humphrey Lyttelton Band was the main musical attraction that evening. There were also two supporting groups, the Roger Fleetwood Quintet from the BBC Northern Variety Orchestra and the Rhythm Club Band. Our line up was trumpet, trombone, alto sax, tenor sax (both reedsmen doubling on clarinet), piano, guitar, bass and drums. I don't know whether it was an instruction from the organisers of the ball or an idea of the band members but we were supposed to perform in formal attire for that special occasion.

I possessed no evening dress suit and wasn't prepared to pay for the hire of one. As the drummer tended to be hidden at the back of the band, it was agreed that my light grey lounge suit would be acceptable and I borrowed a clip-on bow tie from my landlord to match the appearance of the rest of the band as far as possible. While I greatly enjoyed this special occasion, it was frustrating to have one of Britain's

The Liverpool University Jazz Band playing in the Gilmour Hall, Friday 13 March 1959. The musicians are Dick Wensley (trumpet), Pete Foreshaw (trombone), Keith Allcock (alto sax), Tony Teale (tenor sax), Brian Kennedy (piano), Ron Lloyd (guitar), Brian Hudson (drums) and an unidentified bass player. (Reproduced with the permission of Simpson's Photographic Services, Liverpool)

foremost jazz bands playing in an adjacent hall, yet have little opportunity to see and hear 'Humph' and his men in action.

Among the famous bands and musicians I did hear in the Liverpool University Students' Union were some of those who came to play at dances and others who performed concerts organised by Rhythm Club. I have a vivid memory of Liverpool-born George Melly, singer with Mick Mulligan's Band, performing on the Stanley Hall stage. Melly appeared dressed in a tight black sweater and black jeans and his rendition of *Frankie and Johnny* brought roars of appreciation from the dance floor. As he sang this song of love, betrayal and revenge, he dramatised the performance with facial expressions and gestures. At one stage in the song, he turned his back on the audience and clasped himself in an embrace, his white hands clearly visible moving up and down over his black-clad back and buttocks as he writhed there, suggesting a passionate encounter between Frankie and Johnny.

UNIVERSITY OF LIVERPOOL
GUILD OF UNDERGRADUATES.

FACULTY OF SCIENCE.

Ball

TO BE HELD IN

THE STUDENTS' UNION

2, BEDFORD STREET NORTH, LIVERPOOL, 7,

FRIDAY, MARCH 13, 1959   8-30 p.m. —2-0 a.m.

*Liverpool University Science
Faculty Ball ticket (front), 1959.*

Programme

STANLEY HALL.

DANCING 8-30 P.M. — 2-0 A.M.

to

HUMPHREY LYTTLETON AND HIS BAND

and

THE ROGER FLEETWOOD QUINTET
(*from B.B.C. Northern Variety Orchestra*).

GILMOUR HALL.

DANCING

to

THE ROGER FLEETWOOD QUINTET

and

UNIVERSITY RHYTHM CLUBS.

REFRESHMENTS.

11-00—12-00 IN THE DINING ROOM.

SOUP 1-45 a.m.

FILM SHOW   11-00—11-30.   11-30—12-00.

BARS.   MEN'S LOUNGE AND WOMEN'S LOUNGE.

CAR PARK : UNION CAR PARK.

CARRIAGES — 2-15 a.m.

*Liverpool University Science
Faculty Ball programme, 1959.*

The bands hired for Union dances usually played traditional or New Orleans/Dixieland jazz. Indeed, at that time the so-called 'Trad Fad' had reached its peak. The British popular music world was dominated by bands such as those of Chris Barber, Alex Welsh and Acker Bilk. A jazz offshoot known as 'skiffle' was popularised by Lonnie Donegan, who became an influence on many youthful groups – including The Beatles.

Rhythm Club musicians, too, played 'trad', but their interests went far beyond that, something which was clearly reflected in their playing. Increasingly, the influences of swing, even modern jazz could be seen in the instrumentation and heard in the music. The band that played at the Science Faculty Ball could be classed as 'mainstream', strongly influenced by the swing bands of the 1930s and '40s. The later Rhythm Club Quintet comprised vibraphone, piano, electric guitar, bass and drums, the influence of George Shearing being obvious. Our guitarist at this time was Gus Craik, a Scots research student who eventually became Professor and Head of the Psychology Department at the University of Toronto, achieving an international reputation for his work on memory and ageing. Contemporary with this quintet was The John Rotherham XI, a band named, at my suggestion, after the talented and influential engineering student from St Helens who became Rhythm Club's musical director in 1960. This unusual student jazz orchestra comprised two trumpets, two French horns, alto, tenor and baritone saxes, piano, guitar, bass and drums.

Inspiration came not only from records and local musicians. While at Liverpool, I went to concerts given by some of the jazz greats, including Kid Ory, George Lewis, Count Basie, Duke Ellington, Woody Herman, Miles Davis, Thelonius Monk, Art Blakey, Gerry Mulligan, Dave Brubeck and the Modern Jazz Quartet, while visits by the Jazz at the Philharmonic outfits enabled me to see and hear stars such as Roy Eldridge, Dizzy Gillespie, Coleman Hawkins, Stan Getz, Shelley Manne, Jimmy Giuffre, Sonny Stitt, Oscar Peterson and Ella Fitzgerald.

On visits to London I attended concert performances by Basie, Ellington, Brubeck, Gillespie, Buck Clayton, George Shearing and others. And I went to the famous Ronnie Scott's Clubs to hear Dexter Gordon and Art Farmer. The omission of Liverpool on Louis Armstrong's 1959 British tour meant a Rhythm Club coach trip to Manchester's Belle Vue in order to see the ageing jazz genius.

Many of the leaders of British modern jazz performed in Liverpool, not only at The Cavern, but also at the University. In this I played a role of which I am proud. The University's Rhythm Club had a close relationship with The Cavern. It advertised Cavern events on its noticeboard in the Union and its members were admitted to the city's leading jazz club at a reduced price. This arrangement was in place when I joined Rhythm Club but, when I became a member of the committee, I also negotiated with The Cavern manager to have visiting jazz bands play lunchtime concerts in the Students' Union at relatively little cost. I suppose for the visiting bands their performance at the University was a practice session, but for those of us in Rhythm Club it was a wonderful opportunity to meet and hear some of Britain's top modern jazz musicians. These included Dill Jones, Tony Kinsey, Bill Le Sage, Tubby Hayes and Ronnie Scott.

I remember particularly the arrival of the Jazz Couriers at the Students' Union. Led by tenormen Tubby Hayes and Ronnie Scott, this was one of Britain's foremost modern jazz groups. They seemed disgruntled because there had been no one outside to meet them, and as they came through the Mount Pleasant entrance, where a few of the committee members were waiting, I heard drummer Phil Seamen muttering something about being treated 'like a f***ing bunch of f***ing Liverpool semi-pros'.

Our genuine welcome soon smoothed things over and we all went to the Stanley Hall Green Room to prepare for the performance. There, Phil Seamen asked where he could go 'for a piss' but when we told him, he decided that it was too far to go, and made do with a handy wash-basin. I had been having some trouble with my snare drum and I brought it along to seek the distinguished drummer's advice on the matter. His helpful response was, in essence, that I should get a new one. Much as the idea appealed to me, I was unable to find the money to put it into practice.

By this time, The Cavern had become mainly a venue for Merseyside beat groups such as The Beatles, Gerry and the Pacemakers, the Swinging Blue Jeans and numerous others, as well as visiting groups. This meant that I rarely went to The Cavern, although I do have memories of a few jazz evenings there. Particularly exciting was the visit of American tenorman Zoot Sims playing with Ronnie Scott and his band. In a totally different vein, the blues duo of Sonny Terry and Brownie McGhee delighted the audience in a venue where amplified electric guitars, not acoustic guitar and harmonica, were now the norm. On another Cavern jazz night, I saw the Johnny Dankworth Orchestra attempting to squeeze onto the tiny stage. Some of the musicians used an electric shaver to give themselves a quick trim before the performance, plugging in, presumably, where The Beatles and others usually plugged in their guitars and amplifying equipment.

While I was there, Liverpool University remained relatively resistant to the rise of rock music and the Mersey Sound. Jazz continued to reign

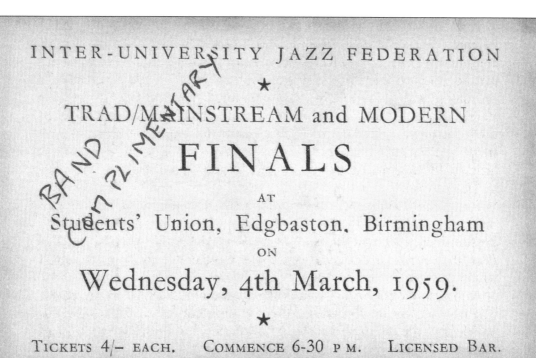

INTER-UNIVERSITY JAZZ FEDERATION

★

TRAD/MAINSTREAM and MODERN

FINALS

AT

Students' Union, Edgbaston, Birmingham

ON

Wednesday, 4th March, 1959.

★

TICKETS 4/- EACH.   COMMENCE 6-30 P M.   LICENSED BAR.

Inter-University Jazz Federation Competition ticket, Birmingham, 1959.

supreme and the Rhythm Club had the largest membership of any of the societies affiliated to the Guild of Undergraduates. Soon after I left the University, however, the influence of rock'n'roll began to reveal itself there. I recall my sense of indignation when I visited the Students' Union and heard young Rhythm Club musicians playing what seemed to me more like rock than jazz.

The big jazz event of the university year was the annual band competition run by the Inter-University Jazz Federation, the IUJF. The competition was held in two stages. The first part, the semi-finals, took place in four regional centres, two in the North and two in the South. The finals were held either in London or a central location such as Birmingham.

One of the 1962 semi-finals was held at Liverpool University, attracting to it student bands and their supporters from northern England, North Wales and Northern Ireland. Liverpool entered two bands, the Rhythm Club Quintet and the John Rotherham XI.

Among my duties as Rhythm Club president at that time was to take the two competition judges, men eminent in the British jazz world, to dinner before the start of the evening's contest. We went to a modest Chinese restaurant. After the meal we hurried back to the Union, now crammed with jazz enthusiasts from all over the British Isles, impatient for the music to start. Without delay, and still wearing the raincoat I had on for my walk to and from the restaurant, I ran onto the Stanley Hall stage to welcome the musicians, judges and audience. I then introduced the young woman who was to announce the bands as they came on stage to perform. Chosen for her glamorous good looks, she wore a little black dress and clearly met with the approval of the male majority in the crowd.

The event was reported in a Manchester University students' newspaper in which comment was made on the charming announcer's pronunciation of bass, as in double bass, which she pronounced like Bass, the well-known brand of beer. I, too, received notice in the report which referred to my opening welcome, describing me as 'a pleasantly nervous man who wore a raincoat and resembled a kind of jazzman's Michael Foot.' I had no objection to being compared to the socialist politician and was happy to see myself later described by the student journalist as 'a tasteful drummer'.

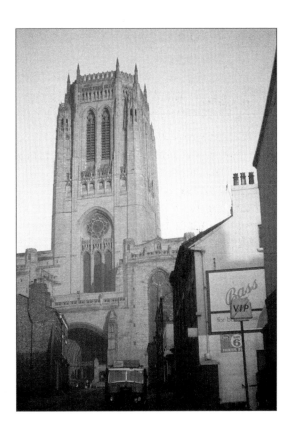

The Anglican Cathedral tower rises above a street in which Bass beer is being delivered to a pub.

Indeed, the Rhythm Club Quintet performed well that night, swinging through its three numbers, the boppish *How's Trix*, the jazz waltz *Little Niles* and a slow ballad, Cole Porter's *All of You*. As we played, we glanced at each other, happy with the feeling musicians get when things are going well, and satisfied that, after all those practice sessions, we were performing close to our top form. It was Liverpool's eleven-piece orchestra that won the day, however, with second and third places being given to groups from other universities.

To avoid excessive duplication of musicians in the two Liverpool groups, we had varied the line up of players. Dick Wensley, who played lead trumpet in the big band, was the pianist in the quintet, while John Rotherham, pianist in the band named after him, played vibraphone in the small group. I had given up my original place in the larger band and let a newcomer take over on drums. Thus, despite Liverpool's success, when it came to the finals at Queen Mary College, London, I was in the audience, not on stage. In the competition final, the Liverpool band was unplaced but this in no way reflected badly on the musicians. The standard of musicianship in many universities at that time was remarkably high and some of those who took part in the IUJF competitions made names for themselves in the professional jazz world. Among them were Cambridge University's Dave Gelly and Art Theman, who led the winning band in the 1962 competition finals.

Liverpool Rhythm Club's activities were by no means confined to involvement with the annual IUJF band competition. There were frequent talks and record recitals as well as the occasional coach trip to hear jazz performances outside Liverpool. Nor did the student jazz musicians and jazz enthusiasts confine their musical activities to the University. University bands played in a wide variety of venues in and out of the city, including colleges and clubs, while some student musicians were members of local bands that were not directly connected with Rhythm Club. Notable among these were the Dave Lind and Dave Stone bands in which fellow geographer Phil Morris played trumpet. These dedicated jazz musicians of the old tradition were good friends of mine and I often went to listen to them in clubs such as The Iron Door and The Downbeat. Occasionally, they allowed me to sit in with the group for a couple of numbers, a generous gesture on their part as they regarded me as too much of a modernist for Black Chicago style bands such as theirs.

I was, perhaps, too much of a jazzman for another Liverpool group with which I was associated for a while. Indeed, I was slightly embarrassed for my jazz associates to know that I was actually playing with a local pop or rock group. Today, however, I am happy to confess that I was an original member of Liverpool's pioneer beat group, Cass and the Cassanovas, thus becoming a minor player in the story of the Mersey Sound.

It was in May or June of 1959 that I first met Cass, alias Casey Jones, alias Brian Casser. I was in Liverpool's Jacaranda Club, where I had just spoken with the owner, Allan Williams, about the possibility of getting some engagements there for the Liverpool University Jazz Band in which I played drums. The Jacaranda's resident group, The Royal Caribbean Steel Band, known to some regulars as The Binmen, were going away for part of the summer, and I saw this as a possible opportunity for me and my fellow student musicians to play at the club. 'Not commercial enough' was the club owner's reply to my proposal. Allan never did show any enthusiasm for jazz, preferring to go into business with the local pop and rock scene. Later, he was to become The Beatles' first manager, or so he claimed.

Disappointed at Allan's reply, I turned to leave. As I approached the door, one of two young men sitting nearby spoke to me and invited me to join them. It was Cass. He was later to achieve fame for his role in naming The Beatles. His suggestion was Long John and the Silver Beetles, a name that John Lennon rejected but which influenced the final choice. Cass's companion was Adrian Barber, later a member of Liverpool's well known group, The Big Three. Eventually, he became a successful recording technician working with groups such as The Cream. Both men were ex-merchant seamen. They had been discussing the possibility of forming a pop or rock group when they overheard my conversation with Allan Williams and decided to ask me to join them as their drummer.

Rock group: a cartoon drawn by the author.

Rock group in a club: a cartoon drawn by the author.

Jazz combo: a cartoon drawn by the author.

Jazz trumpeter: a cartoon drawn by the author.

My initial response was negative. At that time most jazz musicians had a low opinion of pop and rock music and I tended to share that attitude. Some jazz enthusiasts condescended to admit that pop and rock could be pleasantly entertaining but felt that it was 'not really Art, Man!' As a keen jazz enthusiast and aspirant drummer, I was much more impressed by tasteful brushwork than by what sounded to me like a mindless mechanical pounding produced by most rock drummers. Things have changed greatly since then, of course, and so have I. Persuaded by Cass and Adrian, I agreed to think about it. I was also interested in Adrian's offer to share the flat he rented in Falkner Square, conveniently close to the university where I was a student.

Unsuccessful in my attempt to find summer vacation work for the University band, I joined Cass and Adrian to form the original Cass and the Cassanovas. Cass and Adrian both played guitar and we were all supposed to sing, Cass taking the lead, of course. We were still in need of a bass player. This was a constant problem as we were unable to find anyone who was able to fill this role on a regular basis. We sometimes managed to get someone on old-fashioned double bass, at least one of these occasional players being, like me, a university student. We became

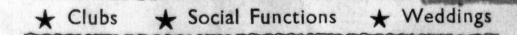

★ Clubs   ★ Social Functions   ★ Weddings

Cass and the Cassanovas

ROCKIN — SKIFFLE — CHA·CHA — POPS
COUNTRY & WESTERN.

188 Vine Street, Liverpool, 7 or Corinthian Club

One of the business cards that Cass had printed for our group, Cass and the Cassanovas in 1959.

a regular band at the Corinthian Club, which paid us £1 each for an evening's performance, 30s on Sundays. The normal hours were 9 p.m. to 1 a.m.

The entrance to this cellar club was reached through a scruffy backyard off Seel Street. To enter, patrons descended a short flight of steps where they were met by a doorman. I remember him as a rather sad, prematurely grey-haired man who used to play one record repeatedly – Nat King Cole's *Mona Lisa*. As far as I recall, the downstairs club was quite neat and clean, not sleazy, as its location might suggest. The music we played was less rock and roll than pop, country and western and, perhaps, rhythm and blues. Of all the songs we sang, I remember only *Sloop John B*, a rather sombre number that had been recorded by the Kingston Trio, and *Old Cotton Fields Back Home*, which we performed with great zest. We rarely knew all the words of the songs we sang, but with Cass's infectious bravado, we managed.

If tall, dark and handsome are characteristics of a man who is attractive to women, Cass scored poorly on the first but did better on the other

The Falkner Square terrace where Adrian Barber and the author shared a flat.

two. He saw himself as a Casanova and women responded accordingly. As a bandleader, he had more modest success. To enhance the group's image, he had us buy identical shirts – tight, woolly, itchy things in the Italian style with vertical narrow red and black stripes. These made us sweat profusely in the stuffy club venues and shrank in the wash. Cass also had business cards printed. I still have one, appropriately coffee stained. Information on the card includes the group's availability for weddings and other functions, as well as its wide musical repertoire, including rock, C&W, skiffle, pop, and cha-cha! Cass's Vine Street residence and the Corinthian Club are mentioned as contact addresses.

I moved into the Falkner Square flat where Adrian lived. There I saw the huge, coffin like amplifiers he used to build at that time. Despite our differences in musical taste, Adrian and I got along together well enough. As the demands of my University studies increased, I had to decide what to do about my involvement with Cass and the Cassanovas. The group wished to continue and achieve commercial success, while I

Falkner Square, Huskisson Street and the Anglican Cathedral tower.

was keen to complete my studies at the University. I also had a strong commitment to the jazz activities there. My break with the group came in late July when I had to leave Liverpool temporarily to do field research on Teesside as part of my university work.

The drummer who replaced me was Johnny Hutchinson, soon to become a highly regarded figure on the Liverpool rock scene. He later became leader of The Big Three when Cass left the group, which then included Johnny Gustafson. Johnny Hutch, as he was known, is probably best known from the famous photograph of the The Beatles at an audition in Liverpool's Blue Angel Club. On that occasion The Beatles' drummer failed to arrive and Johnny was persuaded to sit in with them for their performance. Having no drum kit of his own at the time I left the group, Johnny borrowed mine. When he returned the drums to me shortly after I came back to Liverpool, the bass drum was different. I was told that my drum kit had been damaged in a vehicle accident that occurred when the group was on tour in Scotland with singer Duffy Power. It seems that the bass drum, like the vehicle in which the group was travelling, was a write-off. My original bass drum, like the rest of the kit, had been a very poor instrument and the second-hand replacement was a little better.

A Mersey Beat *front page*. (© Bill Harry, reproduced with copyright holder's permission)

Nov. 2-16

UNIVERSITY JAZZ

by B. J. HUDSON

It is probably a little-known fact that some of Merseyside's most popular and successful jazz groups have among their members students and former students of the University of Liverpool. The Chris Hamilton Jazz Band, the modern trio at "The Blue Angel," and the Dave Lind Jazzmen feature musicians who are, or were, members of the Liverpool University Rhythm Club.

There are, no doubt, many people on Merseyside who think of University Jazz as strangely clad rabble, which, on Panto Day, used to invade Liverpool, armed with trumpets, trombones, saxophones, clarinets, banjos, guitars, drums, and, usually a tuba, from which emanated a sound which, with the widest stretch of the imagination, might be said to resemble that of a New Orleans parade band. There was usually a "second line" to add a touch of authenticity. That this cacophonous assortment of "musicians" is not typical of university jazz cannot be over-emphasised, and there must be many readers who are familiar with seeing Rhythm Club bands playing at dances and other functions at clubs, colleges, schools, hospitals, as well as in the Students' Union and, on two occasions, in St. George's Hall.

A Mersey Beat University Jazz *article.* (© Bill Harry, reproduced with copyright holder's permission)

Cass had something to do with an Arts Ball that was held in St George's Hall. He invited me to participate in this charity event. I remember the feeling of incongruity as I played in that monumental hall, a place better known for oratorios and organ recitals than jazz and rock. A couple of scant entries in my University diaries indicate that I actually played drums in St George's Hall twice, the first time at an Arts Ball on Friday, 15 May 1959, the second at another ball on Friday,

A Mersey Beat Beatles/Litherland Town Hall advertisement. (© Bill Harry, reproduced with copyright holder's permission)

16 December 1960. The band or bands in which I played on these occasions may well have shared the bill with some of Liverpool's top groups, but when the rockers were on I retired to the bar with my fellow jazz musicians.

I left Falkner Square, but continued to live in the area and saw Adrian, Johnny Hutch and Johnny Gustafson from time to time. Cass vanished from the Liverpool scene. Apart from seeing him briefly on a TV show, I recall meeting Cass only once after our Liverpool days.

In the summer of 1962, I was walking along a street in London's Soho when out of a pub ran Cass, greeting me enthusiastically. He had been inside when he saw me walk past the door. Delighted to see him again, I joined him in the pub where, over drinks, we enjoyed catching up with our news. Cass told me that things were going well for him and that he had a business interest in a Soho club, The Blue Gardenia. Hoping to see him again, I asked Cass to write his phone number in my diary, which I have to this day. Unfortunately, there must have been some mistake because when I phoned the number that he had scribbled in my diary, I reached a London police station. The officer at the end of the line seemed pleasantly amused when I explained to him how I came to make this call.

Later, returning from a friend's wedding in Wales, a female friend and I reached London very late one Saturday night, and I suggested we go to the Blue Gardenia Club and see if we could find Cass. It was a nightspot of a kind very different from any that I had previously visited. I had not seen men dancing together before and I was struck by the popularity of mohair sweaters among the club patrons. My enquiries about Cass were not well received. In no uncertain terms I was told that he had nothing to do with the place and that his present whereabouts were unknown. It seemed that Cass and the club had parted company.

I lost touch with Cass and Adrian long ago, but I have happy memories of the short time I was drummer with them. Now I am proud to tell people that I was a founder member of Cass and the Cassanovas, a group that pioneered the Mersey Sound before the Swinging Sixties had even begun.

Merseyside's pioneer role in the popular culture of the '60s was chronicled in a musical newspaper, *Mersey Beat*, founded and edited by Bill Harry, fellow Liverpool art student friend of John Lennon. The paper contained news about Liverpool's various beat groups, personnel changes, venues and performances, as well as advertisements and notices, including announcements of forthcoming popular musical events. I wrote an article for *Mersey Beat*, which it published in the 2 November 1961 issue. It was a rather pompous piece on jazz at Liverpool University. One of the girls who worked at the Jacaranda told me in her broad Scouse accent, 'I liked yer article in *Mersey Beat* – all dem long [pronounced with hard 'g'] wairds'.

CHAPTER TWO

STUDENT LIFE

While much of my university life was involved with jazz and drumming, I was serious about my studies. I attended classes diligently and did all the written and other work assiduously. I could, I suppose, have read more, but I threw myself wholeheartedly into the fieldwork that formed an essential part of both the Geography and the Civic Design courses I did at Liverpool between 1957 and 1962.

For most of that time, and for a couple of years after, I lived within a short walking distance of the University, which lay within a decaying inner city area not far from the centre. Liverpool was the original

The redbrick Victoria Building with the Students' Union on the left.

The Liverpool University and RC Cathedral sites seen from a cleared area to the west.

Redbrick University, the term invented by one of its professors who had written a book of that title under the pseudonym Bruce Truscott. The original core, the Victoria Building, completed in 1892, was a bright redbrick neo-Gothic pile surmounted by a spired clock tower. When I caught my first sight of the building on Brownlow Hill, I recoiled, having been indoctrinated by my readings on modern architecture to regard most Victorian architecture as a dishonest sham. By the time I left Liverpool, I liked it. I am not sure whether this was because by then it had become a more fashionable taste or because I had learned to appreciate the work of nineteenth-century architects such as Alfred Waterhouse who designed the Victoria Building.

For my first three years as an undergraduate, most of my classes were held in the Geography Department which was housed in one of the elegant nineteenth-century Georgian style brick terraces of Abercromby Square. My next two years were largely spent just round the corner, in the Department of Civic Design, which had its own unpretentiously modern brick building. Apart from my first two terms when I shared a room in digs on Campbell Drive, Huyton, I lived close to the University, in Liverpool 7 and 8, much of the time in Chatham Street and, for shorter periods, in Falkner Square, Lilley Road and Percy Street.

Some students lived in University halls of residence out in the leafy suburbs, so, with a touch of undergraduate humour, those of us who lodged in Chatham Street referred to our house in a rather seedy area of the city as 'Chatham Hall'. The house was in one of the terraces on what had been the eastern edge of Liverpool in the early and mid-nineteenth century but which now formed part of the down-at-heel inner city. The houses had been built for the city's middle class but were now occupied by people far lower on the social scale, largely the urban poor, including a transient population of students and other bohemian types such as musicians and painters.

Reasons for living there were its convenient proximity to the city centre and the University, and the availability of cheap accommodation. In a letter I wrote home in November 1958, I noted that I was

The Victoria Building seen from Mulberry Street.

Abercromby Square with the Chadwick Laboratories tower.

Abercromby Square and the façade of
St Catherine's Church, which was gutted by
fire during a Second World War air raid, and
a Victorian pillar box.

Bedford Street South, showing the nineteenth-
century terrace in which Sir William (later
Lord) Holford had his home and office.
The Civic Design Building lies just beyond, on
the corner of Abercromby Square.

managing to live on £4 a week, including expenditure on food, drink, travel, books and entertainment. Of that sum, 25*s* went on the weekly rent.

The area had a significant non-white population – mainly black and Oriental – as well as a variety of other minority groups. Among the shops on Myrtle Street, round the corner from Chatham Street, were a greengrocery run by a black West Indian, a Chinese restaurant, a Greek fish and chip shop and a junk shop owned by a Jew. The West Indian shop proprietor used to arrive in a flashy car, which he parked in the road in front of his premises where he sold vegetables, fruit and a few other food items. He always wore a trilby hat, both outside and in his shop, where he would often lean against the wall, silently observing as the few customers arrived and departed. He had an assistant, a white girl, who attended to the customers. Once when I was there, an old woman entered and asked for a couple of eggs. The shop girl explained

Chatham Street looking towards Sandon Street and Falkner Square.

Chatham Hall: the view from the window of the author's room.

Chatham Hall exterior.

that they did not sell eggs in ones and twos but by the half dozen or dozen. The customer, no doubt having difficulty managing on whatever income she received, pleaded with the shop girl, but the employee, aware that her boss was watching, felt unable to accede to the poor woman's request. Breaking his silence, the proprietor said, 'Sell 'er de two eggs', and the transaction was completed to the satisfaction of all concerned.

Chatham Hall, like the other houses in the terrace, was a narrow-fronted brick residence built in the Georgian style with characteristic sash windows and a doorway distinguished by a fanlight. Five steps led up to the blue-painted panelled wood door with its brass knocker, letterbox and knob handle. The paintwork on the door and the brass fixtures were always kept bright and clean in contrast with the rest of the street. Beside and below the steps was a feature typical of Georgian

View through back window
of Chatham Hall, drawn by
the author.

terraces, a space that gave light to the basement and access to the coal
store beneath the pavement. The front door opened onto a passage to
the right of which were two rooms. The innermost was occupied by the
old couple, Mr and Mrs Walker, whose home it was. Beyond their door
the passage led to the kitchen and the little backyard garden, while to
the left rose the stairs leading to the floors above, and to the attic under
the roof.

During the course of several sojourns there, I lived in different parts
of the house, from the basement, reached by a flight of stairs leading
down from the end of the passage, to a room two flights up and, for a
while, at the very top in an attic room illuminated by a sloping window
set in the slate tile roof. On one winter's morning that attic window was
covered by a layer of snow, allowing a pale, diffuse daylight to penetrate
my little room. In more favourable weather, I sometimes stood on a
chair and opened the skylight so that I could look between the chimneys
across the slate rooftops towards the cathedral tower.

All the rooms were shabbily furnished. The beds, tables, chairs and
other items of furniture looked as though they had all come from cheap
second-hand stores. Linoleum and old carpets on the floor, gaudy
flowered wallpaper on the walls, a gas fire in the fireplace, a wash-basin
in the corner and a gas ring beside it provided a typical room setting.
Furniture might have included a double bed, wardrobe, table, chairs and
other items such as cheap vases and ornaments. At least two of the

Chatham Street: three young residents.

Textures: Chatham Street trees and iron fence.

rooms I occupied at various times had gas fires beside which were what I knew as companion sets, vertical metal stands about knee high, from which were suspended fire irons – a poker, tongs, a small shovel and a brush. These were all useful for tending a coal fire but had no function that I could see in relation to the gas fires beside which they were placed in Chatham Hall. These fires were operated by the coin in the slot system, the meter boxes accepting shillings and pennies in payment for the gas supply for heating and cooking.

Mr Walker, a white haired, bespectacled, wiry-looking man, usually wore bright blue overalls. He always seemed to be busy and the brightly whitewashed walls of the front area and the backyard, as well as the paintwork on the front door and some other parts of the house, gave evidence of his industry. He had been a double bass player in theatre orchestras and once or twice he brought out his instrument to

Myrtle Street on a sunny day, looking towards the Philharmonic Hall in the far distance.

Myrtle Sreet on a wet day. Bedford Stores is on the corner on the left of the street.

demonstrate that he could still play it. It was from Mr Walker that I borrowed the clip-on bow tie I wore when I played at the Science Faculty Ball.

Time seemed to have dealt less kindly with Mrs Walker. As far as I could see, she wore what appeared to be layer upon layer of garments, including a cardigan or two and an old flower-patterned pinafore. On her head she always had a woollen cap of some sort, a thing that closely resembled a tea cosy. Mrs Walker, like her husband, worked to keep the house reasonably clean, but the place was clearly too large for them to look after properly.

Their long life together had been touched by tragedy. They told us that just before the end of the Second World War their sailor son had been killed at sea when his ship was sunk by enemy action. Despite all the trouble we caused, I believe the Chatham Hall students helped fill a gap in the lives of the old couple who had lost their son, an only child, over a decade earlier.

Chatham Hall: a view of the author's room showing the gas fire and its companion set. Note the photographs of jazz musicians.

Chatham Hall: a view of the author's room.

Apart from the half dozen students, there were others in the house; a lone man or two and occasional Chinese residents – seamen, I believe. Mrs Walker used to speak to them in a kind of Chinese style broken English, presumably intended to help them understand what she was saying. The Chinese men were polite and well-behaved tenants and were welcome in the Walkers' house.

With the odd exception, students were welcome too. Rooms were not normally rented to women because the Walkers wished to ensure that their house was seen to be respectable in an area where so many were not. It was for the same reason that male residents were discouraged from bringing in female friends. This presented a challenge. It was difficult to walk past the Walkers' door without a footstep or a squeaking floorboard betraying one's presence. The presence of two or more was even harder to disguise. Even if you made it past their door, there was still the long flight of stairs that creaked under the weight of those who climbed or descended. Tiptoeing did little to help in circumstances such as these and any suspicious sound quickly brought Mrs Walker into the hallway.

Occasionally, as we passed her door, we deliberately tried to give the impression that we were bringing in a guest or two, possibly female, just for the fun of seeing the landlady dash out to confront us. Caught out in her suspicions, Mrs Walker would exchange cordial greetings with us, sometimes picking up a milk bottle as if to suggest that she had emerged to put it on the doorstep for collection in the morning. There were times, however, when she did catch a student coming in with a girlfriend. On one occasion she loudly observed, 'That's not the same one as you brought in last week!'

Women were not the only people who were unable to rent rooms at the Walkers. Black people, too, were unwelcome there. I did not know Mr Walker's feelings on such matters, but his wife made no attempt to hide the fact that, while men with yellow skins were acceptable in her house, those whose skins were black were unwelcome. Mrs Walker often referred disapprovingly to 'them nigs down the road'. Even in relatively tolerant Liverpool, racial prejudice of this kind remained common. When, years later, I took my Jamaican wife to Liverpool and paid a visit to Chatham Hall, Mrs Walker, by then an elderly widow, did not seem to notice the skin colour of the woman I had married.

The Walkers had two household pets, both black. One was a cat with the appropriate name of Sooty. The other was a mynah bird. Like parrots, mynahs are known for their remarkable ability to mimic the human voice. The Chatham Hall bird sounded astonishingly like Mrs Walker, whose voice reminded her student tenants very much of Minnie Bannister (Min), a character in the BBC radio comedy series *The Goon Show*. Once, when I knocked on her door, I thought I heard a reply from Mrs Walker. The subsequent conversation went on for some little time before I realised that I was talking to the mynah. Mr and Mrs Walker were not at home, but their pet bird was happy to enter into conversation with anyone.

Among my student companions at Chatham Hall over the years were fellow jazz enthusiasts, and even, for a while, a tenor sax player in the University band, but these were few in number. Unlike me, some were keen on sport, especially football, and it was through these friends that I learned about a planned coach trip to Aberystwyth, Wales. There was to be a soccer match between teams from Liverpool University and the University of Wales, Aberystwyth, and some of the Chatham Hall sporting types were going along – to play or just watch. Having been told that there were spare seats available on the hired bus, I decided to take advantage of this free day excursion to see a part of Britain I had not visited. The return ride actually cost me sixpence, the amount I contributed to the collection for the driver at the end of the trip.

After a pleasant drive across the hills of central Wales through places with names the English find difficult to pronounce, we arrived at the coastal town of Aberystwyth. On arrival, a friend and I quit the rest of the group, which went off to the football match. The two of us explored the streets and seafront of the little town and were delighted to find that that the shop signs were, indeed, dominated by names such as Jones, Evans and Hughes, as was proper in a Welsh community. Likewise, we were reassured to see vases of daffodils, the Welsh national flower, on the dining tables in the student refectory at the old University College on the promenade facing the bay.

Rejoining our friends after the football match, we went to a local pub to enjoy a few, probably more than a few, pints. There, we were warmly welcomed by a young man who was evidently in charge. Our host explained that he had been a student at the nearby university, but was taking leave from his studies, having recently failed his course. When closing time arrived, he locked the doors, but, ignoring the licensing laws, invited us to stay and continue drinking. This pleasant state of affairs eventually came to an end for what struck me as the most appropriate of Welsh reasons – our genial host had to depart in order to attend choir practice.

Back in England that evening, I felt satisfied that my day trip to Wales had given me the experience of another country, one that was not entirely foreign, but was different enough to be especially enjoyable. Many students at Liverpool University came from Wales and some of them told me that they spoke Welsh as their first language.

Liverpool geography students had many opportunities to visit places of interest in the region, particularly on field excursions associated with their studies. These usually involved coach travel, some lasting a day, others a weekend. There were also the week-long Geography Department annual field trips to more distant study areas, some overseas.

One weekend trip organised by the student Geographical Society took us to Clitheroe and the Ribble Valley. We had managed to book accommodation in a large old manor house owned by the Girl Guides Association. Some senior officers in the Guides were unhappy about our alcohol consumption and the late night return of some of the girls in their charge, who seemed not to mind the attentions of the male visitors.

What I remember most about this trip was the return journey to Liverpool. We made our slow way home through very dense fog, visibility deteriorating as darkness fell. Our driver peered anxiously into the obscurity ahead and was obviously tense and worried as he piloted the coach along the country roads. The beams of the headlights did not penetrate far, their light scattering and becoming diffused in the enveloping fog. After what seemed like hours of painfully slow progress, the driver began to consider stopping the bus and parking somewhere until conditions improved. This could have meant an uncomfortable night spent aboard the vehicle, something that none of the passengers wanted to endure.

We came up with the idea of assisting the driver by having relays of students run ahead with hand-held flashlights that would guide the bus along the almost invisible road. This we did, male students taking turns to run in front of the bus in pairs, each man holding a flashlight directed behind him towards the driver. The arrangement worked quite well, although progress was slow and the driver remained in a state of high anxiety. So slowly travelled the bus that male students found it convenient to descend from the vehicle while in motion in order to relieve themselves. I hold a vivid image in my mind of a line of spectral figures illuminated by the fog-diffused lights of the slowly passing bus as the men peed into the roadside hedge, observed, with great amusement, by the passengers aboard.

When, at last, we reached the fringes of Liverpool, the driver decided that he had had enough. He parked the coach and departed, leaving his passengers to make their own way home as best they could. The streets were almost deserted, and we thought that, in these conditions, the buses might have stopped running. Expecting a long walk home with our small overnight bags, we Chatham Hall residents were soon pleasantly surprised to see a Liverpool Corporation bus loom out of the darkness, heading in the direction of the city centre. The rows of lights on its two decks made it look like a huge, ghostly lantern gliding mysteriously through the foggy night. We hailed the driver who pulled up for us, even though we were not at an official bus stop. To our great relief, we learned that he was going in a direction that would take us close to where we lived. Weary from the exertions of the day, we were happy to return to the modest comforts of our Chatham Street rooms.

Most of the students at Chatham Hall were from the north of England. One of the exceptions came from Surrey, a sin for which he was made to suffer. Another came from Essex, but had such strong Lancashire connections that he managed to avoid censure on this count. He had lived for a while in Poulton-le-Fylde and was a fanatical Manchester United supporter. My Yorkshire origin and obvious love of the North apparently more than compensated for my accent, which betrayed Southern connections. Among us was one student whose strong Leeds area Yorkshire accent was unsullied by any Southern links. His red hair and ruddy complexion matched his aggressively Northern working-class manner. A highly intelligent fellow geography student, he did his utmost to hide a genuine interest in the subject matter of his university studies, dismissing academe and the accepted values of 'cultured society'. His uncouth behaviour became even more outrageous under the influence of alcohol, and he consumed beer (mainly Tetley's bitter from his home county) in vast quantities.

One night, he came with us to a dinner held at The Stork Hotel, a function organised in honour of Liverpool's John Rankin Professor of Geography. We all drank a lot both before and during the meal. Some of us consumed quite a few beers before going to dinner, then, at the table, drank unaccustomed sherry and port, thus adding to the evening's merriment and enhancing our vocal appreciation of the speeches. Afterwards, when we set off from the hotel for our walk home, our Yorkshire pal made an announcement. As many of his old mates back home in Pudsey had experienced police arrest and incarceration some time in their lives, he now intended to get himself locked up that night, just for the heck of it. In vain we urged him to return with us to Chatham Street.

The next morning there was no sign of him at Chatham Hall. We decided to investigate. Heading first to the Crown Court, we learned there that our missing person was in a police cell and due to appear before the magistrate that morning charged with drunk and disorderly behaviour. We found his name on a list posted in a corridor, but it appeared that there was some uncertainty about his identity. Beside the name we recognised as his was an alternative, Brian Ackroyd. It appeared that he had given a false name to the arresting officer, something that we feared would make matters worse. Choosing seats at the back of the courtroom, we faced the bench. There sat three magistrates, a woman with a man on each side of her.

We watched as justice was done, several men, mostly Irish regulars it seemed, being brought in on minor drunk and disorderly charges and fined 10s each. Then it was our friend's turn to stand in the dock. In reply to the question, 'Is your name Brian Ackroyd?' he answered in a blunt Yorkshire monosyllable, 'No'. 'Now he's in trouble', I thought. From a whispered conversation between the three on the bench, I heard the words, 'Is he a student?' Whether this made any difference to the outcome, I cannot say, but a fine of 30s was imposed and that was the end of the matter.

From our friend's account after the courtroom hearing, it appears that his first attempt to be put in a police cell for the night was unsuccessful. Not all Liverpool policemen are keen to arrest drunken students who make rude remarks and gestures at them, preferring instead to advise the intoxicated youths to return home and sleep it off. It was afterwards, on his way back home, that he was stopped by a policeman and taken into custody for drunk and disorderly behaviour. This particular officer of the law was unimpressed by the merry student's lusty rendition of *Great Balls of Fire* as my friend made his way through the city streets. In order to maintain the public peace, the policeman found it necessary to use his leather gauntlets to beat the head of the singing youth, a procedure that evoked the protests of several female passers-by who shouted, 'Geroffim, yer bastard!'

Perhaps it was because of my birthplace, love of the North and interest in jazz that my Yorkshire friend and I got on so well, even though my taste for Miles Davis, Charlie Parker and other modernist musicians provoked ridicule from the staunch traditionalist. He took no exception to my accent or even to my academic achievements. He did comment on my hearty appetite, occasionally enquiring, in his jocular Yorkshire manner, 'Well, 'Udson, 'ow's yer tape worm?'

He eventually wedded 'a mill lass' from his home area, where the couple started married life in a back-to-back terrace house that had survived from the previous century. I was one of those privileged to be invited to the wedding and the traditional pre-nuptial bachelor's night booze-up. I remember how deeply moved I felt when, having accepted the pint I gave him when it was my round, my old student friend looked me closely in the eye and uttered the kindest words he ever spoke to me: 'Well, 'Udson, tha's not such a bad bugger!' For those unfamiliar with British working-class vernacular of that time, I feel it necessary to point out that it was recognised as a sign of true mateship and trust for a man to address another in such insulting terms.

Student life in Chatham Hall lacked refinement, to say the least. This was particularly evident in the cuisine. Canned food, cheap frying steak, sausages, eggs and potatoes were standard fare. Some dishes, such as bangers and mash, were incomplete without the accompaniment of thick brown sauce poured from the familiar bottle that always stood on the table along with the salt and pepper.

At that time many working-class people bought luxury items, such as furniture and television sets, on credit through hire purchase schemes known as HP. Among the popular brands of brown sauce in Britain is HP Sauce, derived from the Houses of Parliament, an image of which appears on the label. At Bedford Stores, on Myrtle Street, the shop girl behind the counter knew exactly what I wanted when I asked her for a bottle of sauce. Here, 'sauce' meant thick brown sauce unless preceded by the word 'tomato'. Tomato sauce was a thick red sauce otherwise known as ketchup. Bottled sauce, the usual brown kind, was what you put on your sausages, bacon, meat pies and, commonly, fish and chips. Sauce went with just about everything. In response to my request, the shop girl propped a ladder against the shelves and climbed to where she could reach the bottled sauces on display. There were several brands, including OK, A1, Daddies and, of course, HP. Naming one of the most popular, the girl asked, 'Do you want HP?' For a laugh, I replied, 'No thanks. I'll pay cash.' The joke was appreciated and the girl turned to the others in the shop, exclaiming, 'Didjerearim?'

The Myrtle Street shops were very handy for Chatham Hall residents. So was the Myrtle Street Hotel, the nearest pub. We became well known there and we got to know the regulars. Learning that we were at the University, some of those who drank at the Myrtle assumed we were medical students and sought our advice on health problems. One of these regulars suffered with his chest, so we gave him the nickname, 'Chest'. Another was a woman we called 'Vingt', French for 'twenty' (the number of children she had had). Not all of her babies survived and thirteen was the highest number of children Vingt had living at any one time. Such was her luck in life. We became quite good friends with some of the younger regulars there. Once we were invited to what they called a 'coming out' party – it was for a mate of theirs who was coming out of prison after serving a term behind bars.

After a few drinks, the pub patrons often broke into song, doing their renditions of some of the recent hits. We used to look forward to the Myrtle Street version of *My Happiness*, a song recorded by Connie Francis and which, sung in this venue, demonstrated Scouse pronunciation beautifully. Starting: 'Evening shadows make me blue', the lyrics contain the line, 'Any place on earth will do', and it was the word 'earth' that we particularly liked to hear, pronounced with great emphasis as 'airth'. A couple of young men who went there regularly sometimes brought along a guitar with which to contribute to the *soirées musicales*. Some might have called these two fellows Teddy Boys, but one should not judge from appearances. Once, when a few of the students in the pub were, for a change, talking about their studies, one of the Teds leant over and said, 'Isn't dat de t'eory of isostacy yer discussin'?' He had been browsing through a physical geography textbook that one of the students had just borrowed from the library and had with him while enjoying a pint or two with friends.

Living so close to the centre of Liverpool, we did not confine our drinking or shopping to Myrtle Street. The big city stores, such as Lewis's, Owen Owen's and T.J. Hughes were within easy walking distance. So was St John's Market, demolished for redevelopment in 1964. There, at a time when Dr Christian Barnard's pioneering work in heart surgery and organ transplants was making the headlines, I once passed a butcher's stall which displayed a topical handwritten sign. On a card among the liver, kidneys and sheep's hearts on sale were the words, 'Get your transplants here'.

The streets and squares that surrounded St John's Market had many pubs, making it an ideal area for a pub-crawl. On nearby Lime Street were several others, including The Vines, one of Liverpool's architectural gems. This was outshone only by the Philharmonic Hotel, much nearer the University. From its ornate entrance, with its wrought metal gates, to its monumental, richly tiled urinals, The Phil is a work of art.

Within the University precinct there was one pub that was particularly close to the hearts of generations of students – Mrs Mac's. It probably had a more official name, but I recall no mention of it. It was a Liverpool pub of the plainest kind, its distinguishing feature being the ceiling on which were scrawled the signatures of innumerable students who had drunk and, no doubt, got drunk there. It was a sad day when Mrs Mac's was demolished to make way for a new university development.

Another student pub worth a mention is Ye Cracke, a place now famous for its association with The Beatles. Being close to the Liverpool College of Art, which both John Lennon and Stuart Sutcliffe attended, Ye Cracke was frequented by art students. It was also popular with other Liverpool students and the place was often so crowded that it was almost impossible to move. Why people went there to drink in extreme discomfort when there were so many excellent alternatives is hard to understand. I suspect that there was a kind of perverse pleasure in being jammed together with other willing sufferers in the narrow confines of the old watering hole.

While many of Liverpool's young artists could be found in pubs such as Ye Cracke and clubs like the Jac, the works of world famous painters and sculptors were on display to the public in the Walker Art Gallery opposite St George's Hall. Apart from its excellent permanent collection, there was the biennial John Moores Liverpool Exhibition of contemporary art and other temporary exhibitions. Particularly memorable for me was an exhibition of Old Masters on loan from the collection of one of the Oxford colleges. One of the paintings was of a

Ye Cracke pub at night. As students at the nearby Liverpool Art College, John Lennon and Stuart Sutcliffe used to drink here. As a student at Liverpool University, so did the author and his pals.

centaur by Italian Renaissance artist Fra Lippo Lippi. This picture clearly fascinated one of two young boys who had wandered in. Gazing in amazement at the image of the mythical beast, half human, half equine, one of the boys called out to his friend, 'Come over 'ere, La. There's an 'orse that's just eaten a fella!'

I witnessed a similar example of art appreciation late one evening near Central Station. A number of Vincent van Gogh reproductions were on display in a shop window. In front of the shop was a bus stop. A Liverpool Corporation bus crew of driver and conductor were waiting there with their double-decker, which was due to leave in a few minutes. Staring into the brightly lit window where cheap colour print copies of *Starry Night* and other van Gogh masterpieces were displayed, one of the men commented, 'The fella what done them pictures must have been f*****g mad!'

CHAPTER THREE

THERE GOES THE

NEIGHBOURHOOD

The iron ball on the end of the chain swung ominously as the crane manoeuvred in front of the brick façade of the building across the street. I watched from the Students' Union steps as demolition workers started to knock down the old chapel which had stood there for precisely one hundred years. The date carved over the entrance was 1857 and it was now 1957, the centenary year of the chapel's opening.

I had recently arrived in Liverpool to commence my studies at the University and I now found myself in a part of the city where all around

The Maths and Oceanography Building from Peach Street.

The Maths and Oceanography Building looms over the doomed 'Mrs Mac's'.

buildings were being torn down to make way for new development. Much of the destruction was to provide room for the expanding university itself. The brick-walled, slate roofed chapel across the road was going to be replaced by a modern steel and concrete Mathematics and Oceanography building, complete with a separate block containing the latest thing in computers. We University students hoped that Mrs Mac's, the pub round the corner, would be spared the chapel's fate, but, like most of the terraced Victorian houses nearby, it too was sacrificed to progress.

The chapel, the pub, the shops on the corner, the once fashionable terraces now largely occupied by university departments, and the humble houses of the backstreets were evidence of an old established community on the verge of final extinction. Dominating the scene was the redbrick neo-Gothic Victoria Building. This was the old core of the University of Liverpool, situated adjacent to both the local workhouse and the lunatic asylum when it was opened in 1892.

The Victoria Building framed by modern University blocks.

The Chadwick Laboratories tower rises over condemned Peach Street terraces.

The Chadwick Laboratories tower and the Architecture Department seen from a cleared site.

Hope Street, showing Hope Hall, the RC Cathedral under construction and the Victoria Building in the distance.

Boys playing football on a cleared site with the construction of the University Students' Union extension in progress.

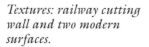

Textures: railway cutting wall and two modern surfaces.

Slashing through the area was the deep railway cutting for the line linking Liverpool with London. The frequent locomotives that rumbled loudly through the dark canyon continually belched forth steam and smoke that enveloped adjacent buildings in noxious dirty white vaporous clouds.

Over the years I spent in Liverpool, the area was rapidly transformed as university buildings designed by many of the country's most distinguished architects and landscaped spaces, created by planners and designers of note, replaced what was once a vibrant inner-city neighbourhood.

The original concrete façade of the Maths and Oceanography Building.

The Roman Catholic Cathedral under construction in an area cleared for redevelopment.

Clockwise from top left: Boys playing football on a cleared site, with Chadwick Laboratories tower beyond; Triple metal sculpture and shadows; Three little girls looking at a pond beside the Maths and Oceanography Building.

It was not the first dramatic change to occur there. Its prosperity founded on trade and commerce associated with sugar, cotton and slavery, Liverpool expanded rapidly in the eighteenth and nineteenth centuries. By the mid-1800s, much of the area now largely occupied by the University had become a desirable residential district with streets and squares reminiscent of some of the more fashionable parts of London. By the time I arrived in the late 1950s, however, the area had declined both socially and physically. It was no longer the respectable and well-off who lived there but the lower end of society, poor working-class people together with some bohemian types who were attracted to the area. While the expanding University breathed new life of a kind into the decaying streets around it, it also resembled a cancerous growth that eventually destroyed the living organism that was the local community.

On 29 January 1964, the *Liverpool Echo* published an article of mine in which I argued for the provision of residential accommodation for

The sculpture and Chadwick Laboratories tower.

students and staff in the area which was being redeveloped for University expansion. In it I wrote:

> At present, the university development programme is depopulating part of the city and creating a district of large buildings and green spaces which dies at night and during vacations. Soon the Pembroke Hotel will follow the fate of 'Mrs Mac's'. The Pack of Cards has gone and No.5 may soon follow suit. Presumably the days of the Mulberry Bush and the Cambridge are numbered.

On a visit to Liverpool twelve years later, I was pleased to see that some student accommodation had now been provided close to the University precinct – Philharmonic Court, just off Myrtle Street. I understand that there is now some on-campus accommodation, including Mulberry Court, the name of which suggests that my fears for the future of one old pub were justified. Happily, the Cambridge survived the redevelopment and now, much upgraded, flourishes as a popular refreshment spot within the University campus.

While students and staff brought some useful business to shops and pubs in the area, the disappearance of family homes and their replacement by university buildings mainly spelled economic decline. Among the businesses to suffer were the barbers. Although the fashion of long hair for men was still some years in the future, male students did not spend much money on their coiffure. Even those who chose to live close to the University did little to keep their local hairdressers in business, something that on occasion led to sarcastic humour. Once, when a particularly hirsute student paid a rare visit to his local barber, the man looked at him and said in an aggressive Scouse voice, 'What do *you* want? An estimate?'

Unlike barbershops, banks probably benefited from the University development. They did their best to entice students to become their customers, presumably in the hope that after graduating they would become well paid professional men and women, the kind of people who would be good for business. With my small State Scholarship grant, I opened an account with Martin's Bank, a Liverpool institution with branches all over the city and around the country. I took my modest business to the Myrtle Street branch, conveniently close to the University and in the area where I lived for most of my Liverpool years. When I eventually left England to work in Ghana and then to do research in Hong Kong, I continued to maintain my small account with Martin's on Myrtle Street. Sadly, the days of Myrtle Street's shops and other businesses were almost at an end. In an aerogramme dated

13 September 1967, addressed to me at Hong Kong University, my bank manager wrote, 'You will, I know, be sorry to hear that the Myrtle Street branch is closing down as the premises have been compulsorily acquired by the Corporation in connection with a road widening scheme.' Redevelopment was about to destroy yet another hub of local community life. The manager went on to say, 'I, myself, am moving to Breck Road branch [near Liverpool football ground] and shall be delighted to continue to look after your account while you are abroad.' I enjoyed that personal touch in those days before Martin's Bank was swallowed up by the faceless banking giant, Barclays.

Not far from Myrtle Street is Falkner Square, where I lived during my brief time with Cass and the Cassanovas. Fortunately, redevelopment has spared this gem of domestic architecture. The low social tone of the area in those days was vividly brought to my attention late one evening while I was walking home along Sandon Street, which leads into the square. As I passed one of the terraced houses, a door was suddenly flung open, spilling light onto the pavement. In the passage at the top of the entrance steps I could see a knot of people, clearly in a state of considerable distress. Responding to a shout for assistance, I went inside the shabby home where I learned that there had been a violent domestic row. It appeared that during an argument with his father, a young man had struck his parent on the head with a cup or mug. I suspect that the vessel was not the fine bone china that might have been seen in that house in former years for the old man was bleeding profusely from the head wound inflicted by his now very worried son. I offered to call an ambulance and set off quickly in the direction of some public telephone kiosks that I knew were at the road junction near the Children's Hospital. As I hurried on my mercy mission, I found myself under attack by a small dog, a family pet from the house I had just left. Clearly, the angry animal saw me not as a friend of the family but possibly the cause of the trouble at its home. Fending off the animal snapping at my legs, I eventually reached the phone boxes and found, to my relief, that one of them was in working order and I was able to make an emergency call.

Another of my nocturnal Falkner Square memories is the sound of bells; not the bells of the Anglican Cathedral just down the road, but electric bells or buzzers of the kind commonly found in large old houses that had been converted into separate flats like the one I shared with Adrian Barber. Several times, when Adrian was away or out till very late, I was woken from my sleep by the repeated sound of the doorbell that served our upstairs flat. Sleepily throwing on some clothes, I would descend the stairs and open the front door to discover a couple in a passionate embrace, the woman pressed hard against the panel of

Bedford Street North, showing the author's first car parked outside his last Liverpool residence. Part of 'The Piazza' can be seen in the foreground.

buttons that operated the doorbells. I can't remember whether it was always the same couple, but each time they apologised for disturbing me. I hope that bells rang for them as, unwittingly, they pressed buttons that roused others with their passion.

While my former Falkner Square and Chatham Street places of residence survive to this day, one of the Liverpool houses in which I lived for a time was demolished soon after I left. It was part of a corner block diagonally opposite the Students' Union and stood next to the railway cutting. Across this dark void rose the Maths Building, built on the site of the former chapel. Most of the ground floors of these old buildings on the corner of Brownlow Hill and Bedford Street North were occupied by shops, but at no. 5, where I rented an upper floor, the ground floor rooms were the home of my landlord and landlady. She, I recall, was a French woman who had met her English husband during the war. In the semi-basement below was a space which the couple's daughter and her boyfriend had converted into a café, but it did very little business.

The Victoria Building reflected in Parry's Bookshop window.

A previous occupant of my flat there was a veterinary student, one of those young men about town who seemed reluctant to graduate because it would put an end to the kind of life he was enjoying at Liverpool. I believe that he was from a well-to-do family so he had fewer financial constraints than most. I once visited him in his flat across the road from the Students' Union and was astonished by the animal skeletons and bones that were scattered around the living room. I envied this man's good fortune in having a flat in the very heart of the University, opposite the Union building. Little did I imagine then that after gaining my two Liverpool degrees and becoming a professional town planner, I would occupy that very same flat. When, long after, I visited the new bookshop that had been built on that site, I could not help wondering where, among all those bookshelves, was the space that had been occupied by my bed in years gone by.

Like so much of the Liverpool I knew, all the old buildings on that corner have long since disappeared. Where dingy Parry's Bookshop formerly stood is the grand modern Blackwell's Bookshop, next door to an equally splendid pub, the Augustus John. I suspect that the latter acquired the licence previously held by Mrs Mac's. Whereas Mrs Mac's presumably referred to a previous licensee of the pub whose official name few remembered, the distinguished British painter Augustus John thus honoured in the name of a public house, taught art at Liverpool University in 1901–2.

CHAPTER FOUR

ART IN THE CITY

Artistically, Liverpool was an exciting city in the late 1950s and early '60s. Among the best-known contemporary local artists was painter and poet Adrian Henri, who lived in Falkner Square, an area in which I once shared a flat with guitarist Adrian Barber.

One of Henri's canvasses, which I saw exhibited in the Walker Art Gallery, was called *Bird Dies in the City*. I think that it was a montage featuring a dead pigeon, which the artist had probably found lying on the ground somewhere. Unless the avian corpse had been treated with a preservative of some kind, this may have caused problems after a while. I last saw Adrian Henri in London in 1968 when he was playing in a rock group called The Liverpool Scene. He sang a composition of his in which he rhymed the name of controversial politician Enoch Powell with the word 'bowel'.

I never saw any paintings or substantial completed work of another Liverpool artist, if such he was, who was often seen sketching in the Jacaranda Club. I knew him only by his nickname, Dyin' Brian. Nicknames were common among both men and women on the scene at that time, Pete the Beat, Blonde Pat and Grotty Jean being others who readily spring to mind. Dyin' Brian was a bespectacled, pale faced, cadaverous looking man who always wore a fawn raincoat that hung loosely over his gaunt frame. The cause of his sickly appearance has remained a mystery to me.

He used to sit in his favourite corner seat in the Jac, quietly sketching on a small pad he kept in his pocket, or talking intensely about art and life to anyone nearby who was prepared to listen to him. He once told me that he regarded his drawings or doodles as comparable with excreta. They were just outputs of human activity, having little or no value in themselves. He certainly did not seem to regard his drawings as works of art and I don't know what he did with his sketchpad when he had filled it with his pencilled pooh.

Once, when I was having a lone meal in a cheap Chinese restaurant, Dyin' Brian came in and joined me at my table. This time the inevitable conversation about life and art was influenced by our distant view of the tower of Liverpool's Anglican Cathedral, which rose beyond the rooftops across the road. The philosophical artist expounded to me his thoughts on the relationship between that ecclesiastical architectural feature and the bottle of sauce which stood on the table between us. It was the usual bottle of sauce (probably HP or OK) that the typical Liverpool diner demanded, even in a Chinese restaurant.

I do not know what, if anything, Dyin' Brian did for a living. He sometimes served behind the counter of a city chemist's shop that specialised in rubber surgical goods, and I once saw him in a small non-speaking part on the Liverpool Playhouse stage. It was a production of *King Lear* and Dyin' Brian was dressed in the black habit of a monk or priest. One day, when he and I happened to be among those passing time in the Jac, in came Adrian Barber, someone we had not seen for quite a long time. Perhaps he had been away from Liverpool, touring with his rock group, The Big Three. In the ensuing exchange of greetings, Adrian shot a glance into the corner where the familiar gaunt figure sat and said, 'Hello, Brian. Not dead yet?' As far as I know, Dyin' Brian may still be on the road to his grave, occupying the journey with outpourings of drawings and words that, for him, were the excreta of life.

Very different in both physique and in attitude to his creations was another artist who frequented the Jac, sculptor Arthur Dooley. He was a big man who held the highest opinion of his own artwork. He was ever on the verge of a 'big deal' from which he would reap rewards that were his proper due. Former friend of The Beatles, Arthur is probably now best remembered for his sculpture dedicated to the famous pop group. Not one of the artist's best works, it included some plastic dolls that Arthur obtained at Woolworth's, a store where he also found a wife. The Beatles monument, now modified by vandalism and theft, is fixed high on the brick wall of a building opposite The Cavern in Mathew Street.

Arthur Dooley at work in his studio.
(Reproduced with the permission of the Liverpool City Council from 'Liverpool '71')

There was a time when Arthur had his studio next door to the Jacaranda in a former gold-beater's premises, but he lived in various other places in Liverpool. These included Upper Duke Street, Huskisson Street and the former Black Bull Inn, an old pub in the suburb of Woolton. When I last saw him, a few years before his death at the age of sixty-four, he was living in a decayed building not far from his old Slater Street haunts. Indeed, while I knew him, apart from his flat in Huskisson Street, just down the road from Falkner Square, all the places in which Arthur dwelt and worked were very run-down and seemed ready for demolition.

A big, burly former Irish Guardsman, PLO fighter and ex-shipyard welder, Arthur started his career as a sculptor in the late '50s. I remember some of his early bronzes as small, highly polished and tactile bottomy female nudes. The first of his exhibitions that I know about was held in the Liverpool University Students' Union in an upstairs space called the Circular Lounge.

Arthur did not have many pieces to exhibit, and he eked out his modest display of bronze figures with odds and ends which included bits of junk, such as bicycle parts that he found on rubbish heaps. There was a piece of cardboard to which was attached a slice of toast with the words, 'Man does not live by bread alone'. Dominating the centre of the room was a tall structure, comprising some timber beams and a few other odds and ends. Beside it were the title and the price: 'Mother and Child – 900 guineas'. With Arthur's connivance, someone, probably Adrian Barber, came to the exhibition and, feigning outrage, demolished the Mother and Child 'sculpture'. This act of well-staged artistic vandalism achieved considerable publicity in one of the national tabloid newspapers.

Generous soul that he was, Arthur was willing to pass on to other struggling artists tips on ways to achieve publicity for their work. Some years later, while he was living in Upper Duke Street, I paid Arthur a visit at a time when an aspiring local artist was staying with him. Arthur's dwellings, though often lacking amenities, usually had plenty of space. He was always prepared to offer a 'kip' to a friend in need. The yet to be recognised painter went downstairs while Arthur and I talked over cups of tea.

The sculptor told me about an exhibition of paintings that was to be mounted at the Blue Angel Club where one of the pictures to be shown was a female nude by his friend who had just left the room. Arthur had thought up an idea that he believed would bring attention to the work of the unknown painter, who had sought his advice. The wily sculptor told me the plan, which involved changing the face of the

Upper Duke Street, where Artur Dooley once lived, looking towards the Liver Building.

nude in the painting. It was not long after our conversation that I discovered that the ploy had worked. At least one national newspaper ran the story of a Liverpool art exhibition from which a controversial painting had been withdrawn because it portrayed HM the Queen naked.

Arthur had no formal artistic training. He spent some time at St Martin's College of Art, London where he worked as a cleaner, but he claimed that a place such as that could teach him 'f**k all'. A card-carrying member of the British Communist Party, he had little time for The Establishment, including the formal education system. In our conversations about the British class system and the alleged oppression of the workers, I pointed out to Arthur how the children of working-class people, men and women like me, were now able to rise in society because of their access to higher education. 'You've been bought over by the system', he replied. Later, I began to appreciate the essential truth of Arthur's observation.

One Saturday afternoon in November 1963, I saw Arthur in a Renshaw Street café, The Griddle, and I joined him at his table. He had just come from a Communist Party ceremony at the War Memorial in front of St George's Hall, and was in a reflective mood. He bought me a cup of tea, clearly wishing to talk. It was quite a long conversation and, when we left The Griddle, we moved on to a café in Central Station for more tea and chat. Arthur explained to me that, as a CP member and a lapsed Catholic, he was not fully accepted by either group or, indeed, in any society.

He got on well with some Catholic clergy and was a great admirer of a local priest who took school leavers to meet various employers to find jobs. He also had a genuine respect for the late Pope John, holding this radical church leader up as an example to be followed, no doubt to the discomfort of those who were happy to see that pontiff replaced by his conservative successor. Arthur told me about a Communist Party lecture he had recently attended, in which an Oxford scholar had talked about Thomas More's *Utopia* in relation to Socialism.

Gleefully, my bluff artist friend described how he had 'niggled' the speaker with his questions. Arthur had suggested that, under the strong influence of the Church, More was interested in 'form, not movement' and thus was inclined to speculate rather than act. For More, our present existence was relatively unimportant when compared to the hereafter. Dooley suggested that the speaker should have mentioned Wat Tyler, leader of the 1381 Peasants' Revolt, a man who wrote nothing but acted on his convictions. The sculptor believed that form should be derived from movement and that movement should not be constrained by a preconceived form. It was his way of expressing the modernist idea of form following function.

Arthur had been invited to give a talk at a Liverpool girls' school and this turned our conversation to education. Again, the self-taught artist was not being original when he argued that children should be taught the process of thinking and learning rather than being stuffed with facts, but the idea clearly excited him. He felt that he would like to put this into practice overseas. He mentioned British Guiana (now Guyana) as a new socialist state in which he would like the opportunity to work. I do not think that he ever did anything about it, however. By this time, Arthur was probably too attached to Liverpool for him to stay away from the city for long, but from his home base he made his Scouse voice heard far beyond Merseyside. For a few years in the early '60s, Arthur Dooley achieved considerable fame as an artist and as a social commentator and critic.

At that time, Liverpool was well known not only for its music and sport – especially its two famous football teams, Liverpool and Everton – but also for its ambitious city centre redevelopment plan. The greatly publicised urban renewal scheme involved massive ring road construction, the creation of an extensive system of pedestrian routes and spaces, as well as slum clearance and new housing development on a huge scale. Arthur saw this as a threat to Liverpool's working-class communities, and among the greatest villains he identified in the process were the planners. I suppose it is quite remarkable that someone like me, who had chosen a career in the planning profession, could remain a good friend of this scourge of planners, but the two of us got on well for years.

It was during the time when I was on the planning staff of the Skelmersdale Development Corporation that Arthur obtained a major commission for the new Roman Catholic St Mary's Church at Leyland, north of Liverpool. He was one of several artists whose work now adorns the building. Arthur created the dramatic bronze Stations of the Cross that are fitted into the Y-shaped concrete supports for the conical roof.

One Saturday, I visited the sculptor in his Slater Street studio while he was working on these bronzes. Never one for false modesty, Arthur enthused about his work to the dramatic strains of a Wagner LP, *The Flying Dutchman*, an odd choice of music, perhaps, for a man of his political persuasion. He may have inherited the disc from a previous occupant of the premises. He stuck a male figure from Christ's Entombment into a pile of junk on his workbench so that we could admire it together as Wagner's tempestuous music filled the air. Then, taking up a piece of yellow wax of the kind normally used for marking tires, he drew on a sheet of metal to demonstrate the idea he had for The Ascension. 'Like a nosecone', he said, comparing the shrouded figure with one of the well-known products of contemporary space technology. He then put a large tick beside the sketch, marking it ten out of ten in bold yellow numbers.

I was so impressed with some of the bronze figures that I wanted Arthur to make one for me. I was particularly intrigued by the small figure of a little boy standing, feet wide apart, to form a shape similar to the capital letter A. Originally holding an O-shaped hoop, he represented alpha and omega, the beginning and the end, but in Leyland Church he appears holding a news-sheet, a *Liverpool Echo* vendor shouting the latest on the Crucifixion. Convinced that my friend was about to achieve a reputation that would make the price of his work soar, I asked Arthur to make me two copies of the bronze boy holding a hoop. I intended to keep one for myself, the duplicate being an investment to be sold at a profit later. He agreed and I paid my artist friend for the yet-to-be-created bronzes.

The bronze soldier that the author
bought from the sculptor, Arthur Dooley.

As the weeks passed, with no sign of my commissioned bronzes, I began to wonder whether I would ever see anything for my money. Arthur was not known as someone who failed to deliver or let anyone down, but there is a common belief that artists are not always entirely reliable. However, eventually Arthur did give me something for my money, something that continues to give me much pleasure, even though it is not what I asked for. One day, I was walking down Slater Street, on the pavement opposite the Jacaranda, when I saw Arthur Dooley across the road. Spotting me, he shouted, 'I've done yer a soldier – f*****g great!'

Prominent among the bronze figures that represent the Stations of the Cross at Leyland are the Roman soldiers who participated in the Crucifixion. Standing stiffly erect with their spears and shields, these are literally faceless images of militaristic power. With heads like tank turrets and crested like proud farmyard cocks, to use Arthur's own analogies, they have flat, polished surfaces where their faces should be. They act as mirrors, reflecting our own faces when we look at them closely. The original bronzes that Arthur made for the church had been given a green patina, an artistic effect produced by the deliberate application of acid to the metal surfaces. Apparently, the church authorities disliked this treatment, preferring the bright, shiny appearance of polished bronze. This meant that the sculptor had to do a lot of work removing the patina and polishing the newly exposed metal.

There was something else that gave offence. On at least one Roman shield was a swastika. Arthur was correct in arguing that this was a Roman symbol long before its appropriation by the Nazis, but no swastikas were to be allowed in St Mary's Church, Leyland. The bronze soldier Arthur had for me was covered in a green patina – with the exception of its polished mirror face and the shiny swastika that adorned the shield. It represented 'f*****g fascist oppression'.

Mine is not the only one of Arthur's bronze soldiers to be found outside Leyland Church. Several castings were made and received different finishes, at least one with, and others without, the patina. Some are in private collections. I believe that one was purchased by Liverpool's Walker Art Gallery. I do not know whether any but mine has a swastika on the shield. I know that it makes some visitors to my home a little uncomfortable and my wife, while sympathetic to the artist's anti-imperialistic motives, objects to having it prominently displayed. Today, I keep it in my study at home, bringing it out only occasionally to show guests.

When Arthur had finished making the bronzes for the church, he asked me if I would be willing to transport the pieces to Leyland in my newly acquired old car. I was happy to accede to his request, although a little concerned about the effect of such a heavy load on my ageing vehicle. Together, Arthur and I visited Bagnall's Foundry, Kirkby, where the casting work had been done and the finished pieces were stored. We decided that the sculptures could be fitted into the boot and back seat and that the old Hillman Minx should be capable of conveying the heavy load as far as Leyland.

I was apprehensive when we set off a week later with Arthur's bulk filling the front passenger seat and the back of the car weighed down with bronze artwork. We arrived at Leyland without mishap and unloaded the sculptures at the church. I cannot say whether it was an effect of the outward journey, but on the return trip to Liverpool my old car broke down. Arthur and I managed to push it to a service station where the fault was quickly identified and remedied. We returned home without further incident.

Soon after, Arthur and I went on a much longer trip in my car; a journey to Yorkshire that was inspired by an invitation made by grateful Catholic Church representatives to the sculptor who had created the Stations of the Cross at Leyland.

When Arthur told me that some Benedictine monks associated with Leyland had invited him to visit them at their abbey in Ampleforth, I thought that it might be fun to drive him there. It would also be an opportunity to show him the Yorkshire countryside I loved. My plan included a brief visit to an aunt of mine who lived in Skelton where I was born. Our route took us through Skipton, where we stopped for lunch in a local café. Some patrons seemed to recognise Arthur, who was by now quite well known in the media.

When we reached Ampleforth, we had no difficulty finding the large complex of stone buildings that comprise the abbey and its associated public school. I drove into the main entrance, and parked the car. Arthur and I then ambled up to the heavy wooden door and knocked. A man in monastic habit opened the door and we explained to him the reason for our arrival. We had not written or phoned in advance about our intention to visit the abbey, so there was a little coming and going of similarly clad inmates before the two of us were welcomed inside. Everything went smoothly as soon as our arrival was made known to one of the senior monks who had met Arthur Dooley at Leyland. Once we were within the abbey walls, we were made very welcome. The monks of this secluded community were delighted to have such an unexpected diversion.

They showed us to comfortable rooms, where we were invited to spend the night, and entertained us with drinks and lively conversation in some kind of common room. The discussion ranged over topics such as the purpose of art and the common goals of Christianity and socialism. I remember a meal in the refectory, a spacious hall with Gothic arches like something out of the history books. We, like the monks, ate in silence while one of the Brothers read from a sort of pulpit. We were informed that these mealtime readings were normal, the texts being chosen from the Bible or other works of a religious or moral nature. As we were escorted along the corridors of the rambling Victorian building, we sometimes heard the chanting of monks in the chapel. During our short stay, we were shown some works of art within the abbey building. These included a carving of the Virgin Mary. With an air of critical condescension, Arthur said of this work, 'Very nice, but it's not Our Lady, is it?'

Having enjoyed the overnight hospitality of Ampleforth Abbey, we bade a grateful farewell to our monastic hosts and departed in my car, heading across the North York Moors in the direction of Cleveland. I was looking forward to seeing again the beauty of Bilsdale, which I had seen before on my teenage bicycle tours. I wondered what Arthur's response might be to the landscape. We drove mainly in silence. Arthur was in a pensive mood, making only the occasional comment about the hidden significance of some remark or other made by the monks at Ampleforth.

When we turned a corner and suddenly saw Bilsdale spread out below and before us, a patchwork of fields cradled in moorland hills, Arthur was moved to speak: 'That must be the most beautiful view in England.' That said, he lapsed again into reflective silence. We arrived in Skelton later in the morning and my Aunt Peg, evidently happy to have this unexpected visit from her nephew and his artist friend, invited us to stay for Sunday lunch.

That evening, Arthur and I were back in Liverpool. At the time, Arthur was living in Huskisson Street where he had a flat in one of the old terraced houses. Once, when I visited him there, he drew my attention to the white painted walls of his bed-sitter flat. Arthur told me that the room had previously been decorated in very bright colours, the work of an art student, but my sculptor friend had found this unbearable to live with. He had the walls repainted, preferring the cool calmness of his present, mainly white, colour scheme.

Communist Arthur Dooley's views on Christianity and his work for the Catholic church in Leyland were the subject of an illustrated feature article in the *Daily Express*, one of Britain's most conservative popular newspapers. I suspect that it was not so much Arthur Dooley the artist and social commentator as Arthur the Liverpool character who attracted the attention of the media at a time when almost anything to do with the Mersey Scene was newsworthy. Less surprising was an article in the left-wing daily, the *Morning Star*, in which a photograph of a pensive

Morning Star *newspaper cutting with a photograph of sculptor Arthur Dooley.*
(Reproduced with the permission of the *Morning Star*)

Arthur appeared with the words, 'He's no pet poodle of the upper class'. For a while he was on some kind of TV panel show. I saw one broadcast in which a fellow panellist uttered profuse words of praise for the sculptor whom he had, so he said, previously misjudged. At the end of this impromptu eulogy, Arthur leaned towards the speaker and, in a loud Scouse stage whisper, said, 'I'll see yer alright after.'

There was even a *This is Your Life* featuring Arthur Dooley, one of the highest accolades that British TV can confer on a celebrity. I was on a visit to Liverpool in early 1970 when Arthur told me about the show, which was scheduled to be broadcast in a few days' time. This was something I didn't want to miss and when I watched it I was not disappointed.

One of the problems that Arthur Dooley posed for television producers was his frequent use of what is commonly referred to as coarse language. He had a particular liking for the four-letter 'f' word. It is a word that gains a special flavour and force when pronounced the Scouse way. The TV show opened with presenter Eamonn Andrews standing in front of the Houses of Parliament explaining that tonight's guest was not a statesman or politician, but an artist. This celebrity was under the impression that he was going to attend an exhibition of Dooley's work held in a room of the famous building in the background.

When the burly figure of Arthur Dooley emerged from the car that drove up beside the well-known presenter, the latter said, 'Hello, Arthur! Do you know why I'm here?' Dooley's reply was typically brusque: 'F****d if I know!' This was the first of many blanked-out utterances with which Arthur embellished the programme that followed, his unacceptable words being replaced by frequent beeps.

When I left England to work as an overseas academic, first in Ghana, then in Hong Kong, I kept in touch with Arthur Dooley by the occasional letter. His replies were brief but always friendly. In one he offered me a 'kip' for when I next visited Liverpool. In another he wrote, 'Hope you are making out with the Chinese birds.' I wish I could remember what I wrote to elicit the following response from Arthur: 'I agree – forward with the Revolution'.

After academic pursuits in Africa and Hong Kong and a brief period as a schoolteacher in Jamaica, I returned to England for a couple of years, accompanied by my Jamaican wife, Anne. Before returning to work as a planner in a London firm of consultants, I took my young wife on a tour of Britain, which included a visit to Liverpool. There we called on Arthur Dooley, at that time living in a former pub, The Black Bull, in the suburb of Woolton. By then, Arthur too was a married man, or had been. I do not recall meeting his wife, Jean, when Anne and I turned up on his doorstep that summer in 1968. I was pleasantly surprised, however, to find that he had another visitor at the time of our arrival; Allan Williams, former owner of the Jacaranda and Blue Angel Clubs and the man who claimed to have been the first manager of The Beatles. Allan was just leaving, holding a small bronze figure of his own creation. *A Diver*, I think they called the crude manikin. Arthur, it seems, had been giving him instruction in making bronzes.

I was delighted to introduce my wife to these old Liverpool friends of mine, and Arthur took an immediate liking to the young Caribbean woman I had married. He would later remember me as the mate of his whose wife was 'dat Jamaican bird'. Anne met him once more during our two years together in England. This time it was on a trip to Liverpool with a couple of friends, accompanied by our son, then not quite five months old. After Anne and I returned to Jamaica with baby Dominic some months later, I lost touch with Arthur Dooley over the years spent in the Caribbean.

In 1985 my family and I migrated from Jamaica to Australia and, a couple of years later, when I was planning a visit to England, I decided I would like to see Arthur Dooley again. I had no idea where he was living at the time but I thought it very unlikely that he had left Liverpool. To help me find him I sought the help of my friend Dave Twiss, a Liverpool architect who lived and practised for some time in Jamaica and Barbados. Dave had returned to England and was working in an office on Bold Street, Liverpool, just round the corner from Slater Street, one of Arthur Dooley's old haunts.

Dave had his own memories of the communist artist whose religious sculptures can be seen in several churches, including Liverpool's Metropolitan Cathedral of Christ the King. As a young architect, Dave worked for a Liverpool firm that had been invited to design a new church building. A meeting was called at the architects' office for discussions involving, among others, officials of the Roman Catholic Church. On Dave's initiative, sculptor Arthur Dooley was also invited to attend. By the time the meeting was scheduled to begin, the architects and Church representatives, including one with the title 'Monsignor', were sitting round the table. Only Arthur Dooley was absent. As time went by, an embarrassed and anxious Dave decided to look outside and, opening the street door, found Arthur sitting on the steps in conversation with a couple of Liverpool 'dolly birds'. Feeling relieved, Dave hurried the bulky sculptor into the meeting room to join the assembled architects and Church dignitaries. Arthur glanced round at the faces which were all turned towards him as he entered and immediately made his position clear: 'Let's get this straight for a start', he pronounced in his aggressive Scouse voice, 'I'm not doin' no more f****n' crosses!' Stunned silence all round.

Years later, my architect friend was again searching for Arthur Dooley, this time at my request. It took only a few enquiries to discover that the sculptor was still living and working in the area just round the corner from Dave's office. On a December day in 1987 I found an older Arthur sitting with a mate of his in a café, part of an old brick building in which he and some other artists and craftspeople had rooms. I sat down at his table and we had cups of tea and bacon butties while we caught up with our news.

He was still working and still confident that he was going to secure that 'big deal' commission which he had always been expecting over the years I had known him. Afterwards, he showed me where he lived and worked and introduced me to his son, Paul, a young man in blue overalls. Arthur took a copy of a book from a shelf and gave it to me. It was John Willett's *Art in a City*, a 1960s account of the Liverpool art world. Arthur Dooley is one of the artists discussed by the author and among the plates in the book is one showing a group of bronze figures from the Leyland series. Arthur did not sign this volume, but he did write on the back of a small, framed colour photograph of another of his Leyland sculptures, a gift to Anne and me. That was the last time I saw him. A few years later, in 1994, someone in England sent me a cutting from the *Independent*, an obituary for Arthur Dooley. It was written by Fritz Spiegl, formerly principal flautist with the Royal Liverpool Philharmonic Orchestra and founder of Scouse Press.

CHAPTER FIVE

LOVE ME DO

For The Beatles and their fans, 1962 was a very important year. January saw the issue of the first commercial record bearing the name of the then little known Liverpool group. On that disc, recorded in Germany the previous year, The Beatles accompanied Tony Sheridan singing *My Bonnie*, a traditional song often thought of as a nursery rhyme. On the other side of the 45rpm Polydor single was *The Saints*, a tune mainly associated with traditional jazz bands. The choice of these two songs no doubt avoided the expense of composer royalties. Recorded in London on 11 September 1962 and released by Parlophone the following month, Lennon and McCartney's *Love Me Do* was the first of The Beatles' discs to be issued under their own name. It got into the British top twenty charts, peaking at number seventeen.

Perhaps during those weeks I became aware of this early success. After all, I knew of The Beatles in Liverpool, and any news about Merseyside and Merseysiders was of interest to me in those days. At that time, however, I was having to come to terms with important changes in my life. My student days had ended and I had to decide what to do next. Then came an unexpected blow. I experienced the bitter taste of death.

Such thoughts were far from my mind when, one evening in 1959, I descended the narrow stairs of Liverpool's Jacaranda Club. From the dark, sweaty basement below came the sweetly metallic sounds of Caribbean steel drums. The resident musicians, styling themselves The Royal Caribbean Steel Band, were a group of local West Indian men who played instruments that they had made out of old oil drums. This was an art that had developed in Trinidad during the Second World War, West Indian migrants bringing it to Britain in the following years. Although, since my Liverpool days, I have heard steel drums, or pan, played in various parts of the West Indies, including Trinidad itself, for me the sound of pan music still evokes mainly Merseyside memories – the crowded darkness of the Jacaranda basement rather than the sunny skies of the Caribbean.

Upstairs in the Jac, as the club was known, patrons could hear very well the exotic sounds of the steel drums being played immediately below them. It felt as though the throbbing music was being transmitted through the wooden floor into your feet as well as your ears. People could listen to the music while sitting in relative comfort, sipping their coffee and chatting with friends without paying to go downstairs. Those who paid their money to Beryl, the Chinese wife of club owner Allan Williams, did so for the privilege of being able to dance to the music.

In truth, there was usually little room for dancing in the Jac's basement. The four musicians and their instruments took up the whole of one corner, while much of the remaining space was normally occupied by people standing around. This left only a small area where couples could dance. At times the place became almost intolerably crowded, the ill-ventilated, low ceilinged, narrowly confined cellar perhaps more like the Black Hole of Calcutta than a nightclub designed for the pleasure of dancing. It was rarely possible for couples to do more than sway in close embrace, pressed on all sides by others similarly trying to move to the rhythm of the music. That, I suppose, was the point of it all. It was where boy met girl.

Jacaranda basement: a cartoon drawn by the author.

It was in these circumstances that I first met Helen. She had come with a girlfriend to experience what she herself described as the sleazy atmosphere of the Jac, by now a well-known coffee bar and night spot in Liverpool. Helen was a recently qualified teacher who had returned home to Liverpool after her college studies down south. She now taught science at one of Liverpool's many Catholic schools. This much I learned while dancing with her and in conversation over coffee upstairs. It was probably there that she gave me her home telephone number, one that is written in an old diary of mine along with others that had not led to any significant relationships.

Helen and I were to 'go steady', as the saying went, for almost a year. We regularly went out to see a film or a play, sometimes having a meal at a Chinese restaurant or coffee at one the city's many coffee bars. Once we made an excursion to Chester where we took a rowing boat on the River Dee. It was a time when transistor radios had become a craze among British youth and the streets of the old city were thronged with teenagers ostentatiously carrying their prized new toys that blared out the latest pop music.

Shortly after we met, I invited Helen to join me, Cass and Adrian at a barbecue function in New Brighton, an all night party at which we were to play. The venue was Fort Perch Rock, a coastal defence battery built during the Napoleonic Wars. Helen declined, believing that her parents, with whom she lived, would strongly disapprove of her staying out all night. Eventually, after we had been going out together for some time, I was invited home to meet the family.

They lived in the suburb later made famous by The Beatles' song *Penny Lane*, not far from Calderstones Park. I used to go to the house sometimes for a meal or to listen to records with Helen. At the start of our relationship, I was living in Falkner Square where Helen would come and visit me sometimes. My flatmate Adrian and his girlfriend Terry called her 'Teach', short for 'Teacher'. Later, I moved back to Chatham Street, where Helen made the acquaintance of Mr and Mrs Walker.

For the first time in my life I believed that I was in love. We talked seriously about marriage, raising the question of our differences on the matter of religion. It was reassuring to know that Helen felt that my disbelief did not automatically mean that I was destined for Hellfire. I do not think that it was the rock of religion on which our relationship foundered. Helen clearly did not share my intensity of feeling and thought it best for us to part. She made it a complete break, something that hurt me greatly. Later, I occasionally caught glimpses of her about town in the company of another, older man. Much later, after I had completed my Civic Design course at Liverpool University, Helen told me about him and her decision to end that relationship, too.

One day, shortly after the examination results were announced, I was surprised to receive a phone call from Helen, congratulating me on my MCD degree. She had seen my name in the list of University results published in the local newspaper. Soon after, we met in town. There, over coffee, Helen told me about her life since we had parted and her decision to leave Liverpool and work overseas. She planned to go to Singapore and teach in a school for children of members of the British armed forces based there. I was very happy to see and talk with Helen again but my old feelings for her were not rekindled. By then I was again in love, with a Liverpool girl I had met the previous year.

I met Diane at a University dance. These frequent functions in the Students' Union afforded excellent opportunities for young men and women to meet, but many of the male students spent much of the time drinking heavily and singing 'dirty' songs. In some cases, perhaps, consumption of alcohol was intended to boost confidence for dance-floor conquest but it could just as easily lead to unsteadiness on the feet during a quickstep or a jive. Waltzes were rare, for on these occasions the music was usually provided by jazz bands.

The university bands in which I played performed some slow numbers, usually blues or ballads and, with an increasing shift away from 'Trad' jazz, we even included a waltz in our standard repertoire, the gently swinging *Tenderly*. As a drummer in bands that were much in demand for dances and other functions, my opportunities for using these occasions to meet girls were limited. When I did go to dances without having to play drums there were times when I, too, spent more time in the bar with the rest of the lads than in the dance hall.

At Students' Union dances, both the large Stanley Hall and the small Gilmour Hall had live music for dancing. The Stanley was the main venue, the place where the big name band played. The support group, usually the University jazz band, played in the Gilmour, taking to the stage in the main hall when the principal band took a break between sets. The evening I met Diane, the University band had no gig and I was at a Students' Union dance where I was not going to be onstage drumming. It was in the Stanley Hall that I spotted the girl who was to become my dance partner for the evening.

It is not the dancing that I remember as much as the conversation, which focused largely on the occupation of my new acquaintance. While probably most of the women who attended these dances were university students, many were students from teachers' colleges and other higher education institutions in and around Liverpool, or nurses from local hospitals. Officially, people who were not members of the University could be admitted only as guests, and on dance nights the Union entrance was often crowded with young women, outsiders, seeking someone to sign them in. There were usually plenty of young male students willing to oblige.

When I asked Diane what she did, she replied that she was a bus conductress. No doubt I showed my surprise but I tried not to give offence with my enquiries. As our conversation proceeded during the evening, it became evident that my dance partner was a well-educated young woman, one with a knowledge of literature that I would not normally have associated with someone in the job she claimed to do. When I ventured to express this view, I was made to feel a little ashamed of myself by Diane's reply, a spirited defence of bus conductresses that rejected any aspersions on their intellectual capacities. What a snob she must think me, I felt, yet I was not completely convinced. I was utterly intrigued by this very attractive girl who seemed to find me amusing.

As the dance came to an end, I offered to walk Diane to her bus, one on which she was going to travel as a passenger, not as an employee of Liverpool Corporation. Fine drizzle moistening our faces and our thick duffle coats, we walked together past the Cohen Library and on towards London Road and the stop for her bus home to Huyton. This enigmatic girl, around whom – as far as the thickness of our bulky coats permitted – I had put my protective arm, agreed to see me again, giving me her phone number so that I could make a date.

There was a public phone booth in the entrance hall of the Civic Design Building and it was from there that I made the call a few days later. My first attempts with coins in the slot and the pressing of buttons were frustrating. I kept getting the wrong place, although once or twice I thought that I had discovered the truth about Diane's occupation when I reached a school office or nurses' home. With a pang of horror, I realised that I must have remembered the number incorrectly when I wrote it in my diary after I got home on the evening of the dance.

Perhaps the numbers were right, but were written down in the wrong order. I tried different permutations and, to my relief, eventually got through to someone who was not surprised when I asked to speak to the girl I named. There was another slight mystery here. Diane was not the name by which she was generally known to her family, who called her Dorothy or Dot. Diane was her middle name, one that she preferred me to use. In my old diary there is a corrected Huyton phone number beside her name. There it is 'Dot', not 'Diane', but the name Diane, not

Dot or Dorothy appears occasionally in the pages of this diary and the one for the following year.

I do not remember how long we had been going out together before I learned the truth about Diane's occupation. She admitted that she was not a bus conductress, something that I had suspected from the start. What Diane was reluctant to tell me was that she was a schoolgirl. She thought that had I known it when we met, I would not have treated her very seriously and would probably not have asked her for a date. Diane was almost certainly right in her assumptions. It was not the done thing for university students, least of all postgraduates, to go out with schoolgirls.

One of the young men, not a student, who shared the basement flat with me at Chatham Hall, teased me a little when he told me that he had seen my new girlfriend in town wearing her school uniform. I never saw Diane thus attired. Not long after I met her, she left school and continued her studies at Liverpool College of Commerce in preparation for university entrance. She was a Humanities student with an interest in modern languages, French and Spanish.

Although I delighted in Diane's company, at first I still felt a lingering yearning for Helen. I thought that my new girlfriend, attractive though she was, could never mean as much to me as Helen had; but as the months passed, I fell deeply in love with Diane. We used to meet in town and go to films and plays, often ending up at the Jacaranda for coffee. I also took her with me to student parties. We went to jazz concerts together, too, for several leading American musicians performed in Liverpool during that period. Diane came with me on gigs at which the University band was playing. Girls who accompanied the musicians on such occasions were known as 'band chicks' and we were always indignant if ever the suggestion was made at the venue entrance that these young women should be charged for admission.

Once I took Diane to the Philharmonic Hotel to show her the richly ornamented late Victorian pub interior. This is an outstanding example of Art Nouveau, dating from the time when artists and craftsmen who were employed to fit out and decorate transatlantic liners also worked on the design and decoration of some of Liverpool's finest hotels. Surrounded by carved wood, ornate plasterwork and stained glass in one of The Phil's characteristic nooks, we sat chatting over drinks. We admired stained glass of another kind when we went on a cheap day rail excursion to York and visited the splendid Minster, famous for its beautifully glazed medieval windows.

That was not our only trip to Yorkshire together. One holiday weekend Diane and I hitchhiked to Skelton-in-Cleveland, where we stopped for a night or two with my Aunt Peg. Our outward journey from Liverpool took us through sunlit Pennine dales, market towns and villages. By hitchhiking, we attained a series of lifts through Lancaster, Kirkby Lonsdale, Sedbergh and into Wensleydale. We stopped at Hawes and walked to Hardraw Force, a waterfall I had previously visited on my teenage bicycle tours. It was getting late by the time we reached the foot of Wensleydale. Fortunately, we got a lift to Middlesbrough and from there took the bus to Skelton, where we stayed with my aunt for a couple of nights. While there, we walked to Hobdale Terrace where I showed Diane the house where I was born.

For me, life in Liverpool then was a blissful routine, one in which my university studies continued to play a central role but which also revolved largely around Diane and jazz. One evening a week I would catch the bus to Huyton and visit Diane at her home. She lived with her parents in one of those neatly designed pre-war brick council houses that characterise several of Liverpool's outer suburbs. Her father was of Irish origin and it was probably from him that Diane gained the soft lilt in her voice. Her parents were charming people who made me feel welcome and comfortable.

At one time, when I was again flat hunting, they put me up in their home for a few days. On my weekly visit, they left us alone in the front room where Diane and I would embrace to the sounds of jazz played on a portable record player. Meanwhile, her parents listened to the radio or watched TV in the next room. At a fairly predictable time, there would be a discreet knock on the door and Diane's mother would enter bearing a tray of tea and biscuits. Later, Diane and I would kiss goodbye at the front door, a ritual that was prolonged by unwillingness to part. This often resulted in my having to run down the road to the bus stop to avoid missing the last service back into the city.

Diane had an elder sister, Norma, a recent graduate of Manchester University. I first met her when I accompanied Diane to meet her sister's train at Lime Street station. When Norma married a few months later, I was one of the few guests at the wedding, a function kept very small at the request of the bride and groom.

Immediately after the reception, Diane departed for Spain, where she spent the summer vacation as a shop assistant. The main purpose of this was to become better acquainted with Spanish culture and more fluent in the language. In order to earn money and to gain some professional experience, I took a summer job in London County Council's Planning Department. At this time, some old friends and I arranged a short motoring holiday on the Continent, driving from Belgium, through France and Andorra, to Spain. Of the five of us who were to pack into the hired car, only one could drive. This was John, a former cycling companion of mine and fellow actor in our Bromley Grammar School dramatic society. His girlfriend, Sylvia, was coming with us, as was another old school friend, David, a dealer in fine art, and his young Sri Lankan wife, Elizabeth.

At some stage on this trip, the five of us, crammed into a hired Ford Anglia with a boot loaded with luggage, arrived in the Basque town of Guernica where Diane was working as an assistant in the Perfumaria Arronategui. Guernica is the place immortalised in Picasso's painting of that name, a work that symbolically portrays the horror of the town's destruction by Nazi planes during the Spanish Civil War. Apart from the church, few buildings in the town dated from before 1937, the year of the brutal attack which killed or wounded 1,600 people. During our two or three days there, we drove to the rugged Vizcayan coast and went to see the Basque ball game pelota in Durango. Six adults in a Ford Anglia was quite a crush but we managed with three in the back seat and Diane on my knee in the front passenger seat.

When I got back to England, I resumed my temporary summer job at London's County Hall before returning to Liverpool for my final year at the University. Diane had arrived home a couple of days ahead of me, bringing with her some presents for me from Spain – a glass drinking flask and a 45rpm EP record of Latin American folksongs.

While I was completing my final year at university, Diane was preparing for her university entry. She accepted the offer of a place at London University's Queen Mary College. Shortly after my graduation I returned to Kent, where I was to start work in a temporary job in the Planning Department at County Hall, Maidstone. Meanwhile, Diane had obtained summer vacation work at Woodlands, a small country holiday camp in the North Downs close to my parental home in St Mary Cray. On at least one occasion, she visited this suburban bungalow where I had spent much of my life before going to Liverpool. Just before I started work at Maidstone, Diane and I visited Tonbridge, where we went canoeing on the river as I used to do in my schooldays. Diane's temporary residence in the familiar Kent countryside close to my parents' home encouraged me to make new use of my old bicycle, long left neglected in my father's toolshed.

During my employment with Kent County Council, I lived with my parents in St Mary Cray, commuting by rail to Maidstone. Once or twice a week I cycled to Woodlands to spend time with Diane. After her day's work there, we would go for walks, often ending up at a nearby pub that served beer from the barrel and was lit by oil lamps. It was usually late when we got back to Woodlands. From there I cycled home in the dark, my way through the country lanes lit only by the feeble beam of my bicycle lamp. A couple of times I visited her in south London, where she stayed in the home of her sister and brother-in-law, and we went to the occasional play or jazz concert in town. During this period, Diane went on a trip to Paris. I returned to Merseyside for a month, filling in for a school geography teacher off work ill.

I missed Diane when we were apart and I began to wonder what would happen to our relationship when she went to university. I had yet to decide how I should pursue my career at this stage and I thought that I might find planning work in London in order to be near her. Today, a young couple like us might choose to live together, one in paid employment while the other studied at university. I do not think that such a thought even crossed our minds. The '60s had just begun, and behaviour of that kind was not yet the accepted norm. We both believed that it was too early to make the commitment of marriage.

As we began this new phase in our lives, we agreed that we should both be free to have independent social lives while continuing the close relationship that had developed between us over the past two years. Diane found digs in East Ham, close to Queen Mary College, which is situated in London's East End. During this period I continued my work with Kent County Council, engaged in planning surveys that involved house-to-house interviews and visits to industrial premises.

One evening when I returned home from work, I found a letter waiting for me. When I first read it, I failed to understand the message. No doubt shock caused the confusion. Initially under the impression that it had come from Diane, I realised that the letter had been written by her sister, Norma. Diane had been admitted to the Royal London Hospital, Whitechapel. She had been injured in a traffic accident and was unconscious.

My memory of what happened next remains confused. We had no telephone at my parents' home, so I made calls to the hospital from public phone boxes; I dashed off to St Mary Cray Station, but found that I should have gone to Orpington. From Orpington there were trains that stopped at New Cross and from there a short underground line below the River Thames went directly to Whitechapel. It was a gloomy and seemingly interminable ride under the river but when I emerged from Whitechapel tube station there was the Royal London Hospital, directly opposite.

Entering from busy Whitechapel Road, I went to the reception desk and explained the reason for my visit. A senior nurse came and spoke with me. Her words and tone of voice suggested that Diane's condition was very serious. I was directed to a waiting room where I found Diane's parents. I admired their calm, though they were obviously deeply distressed. They told me that they had been sitting at their unconscious daughter's bedside, talking to her in the hope that the sound of their voices might help bring her back to consciousness. They sometimes went to pray in the hospital chapel.

When I was allowed into the room where Diane lay alone, apart from a nurse who busied herself quietly there, I sat on the bedside chair and began to talk conversationally. It was just everyday chat, including news of friends in Liverpool. There was no response from the girl who lay under the bedclothes, her face showing only the slightest signs of injury. Tubes and wires were connected to the unconscious patient who breathed so gently there.

On the train coming home from work one evening, I saw in a London paper a brief report of Diane's tragic accident, including the usual comment that the victim was 'fighting for her life' in hospital. The fight did not last long.

Diane succumbed to the injuries she received in the accident. She was a passenger in a bubble car, a popular vehicle back then, which was involved in a head-on collision. The driver, a fellow student, was killed on the spot. The two men in the other car were unscathed. The young man killed at the wheel of the bubble car probably chose to purchase this type of vehicle because it was cheap to buy and economical to run. Sadly, its compact and lightweight construction offered little protection in the event of a crash. Seatbelts were rarely provided in cars in those days but I suspect that they would have been of no use in the accident that caused Diane's death.

Diane's parents invited me to the funeral in Liverpool. I did not go. I believe in rites of passage but at that time I did not see the point of witnessing the burial of a corpse, something which, to me, was not the Diane who existed only as a living being, now just a memory. For a while I stayed in touch with her parents. We corresponded and, on my return to Liverpool, I made one last visit to Diane's home. Her mother invited me to stay for lunch, a meal that I found difficult to eat because my emotional state made it hard for me to swallow. In an effort to take her mind off the recent loss of her daughter, Diane's mother took a job in a city café. The place was frequented by young people, many of them students, and this raised such painful memories that she decided to stop working there.

For a long while, I stayed in a depressed state of mind. It may have been the last time I came away from the Royal London Hospital that I stopped and stared into the oily black waters of the Thames at Blackfriars Bridge. The thought of suicide crossed my mind, but very briefly. Life at that moment was painful, but it had to be lived. In the following months I mechanically went about my daily business, a feeling of bitterness warping my view of the world. I resented the happiness I saw on people's faces. I felt it unfair that young people around me were alive, enjoying life, while Diane – my Diane – was dead. It was largely self-pity, of course. Nevertheless, no one could deny that Fate had dealt harshly with my girlfriend, who met her death while still in her teens only weeks after arriving in London to study at the University.

Eventually, I decided to go to the doctor for help. The GP referred me to a psychiatrist whose assessment and suggested remedy struck me as sensible. I was depressed because I had recently had a traumatic experience. Emotions can be controlled by chemicals, so prescribed drugs could help. After taking pills for a few weeks I felt better able to cope with my sadness and began to take a more positive attitude to life. I still missed Diane very much. Many years were to pass before I could bring myself to play again the record she gave me on her return from Spain.

There was another record, too, that I similarly could not bear to hear for a decade or more. It was *Red Bird*, an EP recording of Christopher Logue reading some of his own poems to a jazz accompaniment provided by the Tony Kinsey Quintet. The piece that I found especially poignant was *Tonight, I Write Sadly*. I first heard it at a student party in Liverpool shortly after Helen and I parted. I bought myself a copy, one that, together with Diane's Spanish disc, I still possess. What I found particularly disturbing in Logue's poem were the last lines: 'Nevertheless, I shall forget her, and, alas, as if by accident, a day will pass in which I shall not think about her, even once'. It was a very long time, years, before that day passed for me. I am not even sure that it has yet come.

The winter that followed Diane's death was at times very hard. It snowed both in Kent, where I continued to work with the County Council, and on Merseyside, to which I returned in early 1963 to take up a permanent post as a planner in a New Town corporation.

While still living in St Mary Cray, I was once walking gloomily home from Orpington when a young woman overtook me on the path. Her face seemed vaguely familiar and I thought she expressed a hint of recognition as we exchanged glances. I was reminded of my days at Chislehurst Road Primary School whose familiar Victorian buildings I had just passed down the road. The woman a few yards ahead of me could have been of one of the girls in my class all those years ago when we were preparing for the eleven plus exam.

As these thoughts crossed my mind, I saw something fall from the young woman's shopping bag. I had the feeling that whatever it was that now lay on the ground ahead of me had not got there by chance. It seemed like the old dropped handkerchief ploy, I thought. In my embittered state of mind, my reaction was one of angry rejection. I picked up the fallen item, caught up with the woman, handed it to her with a gruff, 'I think you dropped this,' and marched ahead without further remark.

About this time I began taking driving lessons. Diane had encouraged me to do this, no doubt feeling that I could not depend on a bicycle and public transport indefinitely for our meetings. I continued these lessons on my return to Liverpool where I bought a car that had had several previous owners. It was a black Hillman Minx that cost me £90. Once I had passed my driving test and received my full licence, I used my car to drive to and from work at Skelmersdale, the site of the proposed New Town. Liverpool, where I continued to live, was full of memories of Diane. It also had many memories of my student days, now sadly left behind.

After another short sojourn at Chatham Hall, I moved to a larger and more convenient flat, an entire floor of an old terraced house directly opposite the Students' Union. The University Bookshop occupies the site today. When I went into the Union building to see if any of my old friends were around, I was greeted with some surprise by one or two who had heard that I was dead. It appears that they had read or heard news of Diane's accident and had assumed that the driver killed in the collision was me.

Now a member of the nation's regular workforce, I began to accustom myself to the routine of commuting between my city home and my semi-rural office, finding diversion with colleagues and friends in the evenings and at weekends. The group of musicians with whom I used to play had broken up and I had sold my drums. I continued to frequent my old haunts, however. The Jacaranda, Blue Angel, Green Dolphin, Iron Door, and the Downbeat were among the places where I used to hang out.

At the Jacaranda there was a waitress whose looks and demeanour attracted me. In some ways, Jane was very much part of the Liverpool scene of the early '60s. In her evening job at the club, she inevitably met many of Merseyside's top musicians and others associated with the local music and art world. She was popular both with the staff at the Jac and the regular patrons, always friendly but not as brashly outgoing as some.

Jane knew me as one of the regulars who came for coffee and the occasional light meal, lingering to talk with the interesting characters that tended to gravitate there.

When she was not busy serving customers, Jane sometimes sat and chatted with me. It was on one of these occasions that I took the opportunity to ask her out. The famous Ballet Rambert was visiting Liverpool and I invited Jane to accompany me to a performance of *Les Sylphides*. We enjoyed our evening together at the theatre, where Chopin's romantic reverie was followed by the contrasting performance of a lively modern ballet.

This was the beginning of a relationship, which, though short and less intense emotionally than others, was beautiful in its own way. By this time, however, I had not long to stay in England. When I finally left my last Liverpool home, I took from my pocket a tiny carved wooden mouse – little bigger than an acorn – that Diane had given me in the Jacaranda. She had told me nothing of its origins or its significance, but I carried it with me always. Just before leaving the house, which I knew was soon to be demolished, I hid the little token over a passage doorframe. I hoped that when the building was knocked down, the mouse would be lost in the rubble and, perhaps, be buried on the site or at some other spot in Liverpool.

Shortly before I was due to leave England, Jane joined me in London, where we had arranged to meet our Liverpool sculptor friend, Arthur Dooley. Arthur was negotiating to have an exhibition of his work at the Grosvenor Gallery, Davies Street, in London's fashionable West End, and Jane and I were to accompany him at his various meetings. The three of us paid a visit to jazz vocalist George Melly in his Hampstead home. Arthur had sold one or two of his pieces to the Liverpool-born singer and they had some further business to discuss. It was probably the same sort of thing that took us to Hampstead's well-known pub, Jack Straw's Castle, to meet BBC TV announcer, Peter Hague. Liverpool art, like its popular music, was beginning to attract enormous attention in London and around the world. It was a phenomenon I was to follow in the news while living overseas.

With the death of Diane, there was little to prevent me from realising my long-held dream of extensive overseas travel. I applied for a Commonwealth Scholarship to Hong Kong and for a university post in Kumasi, Ghana. As things turned out, I was successful in both and spent nearly a year in Ghana before going on to Hong Kong.

A few days after Jane, Arthur and I said goodbye in London, I was in Africa.

Winter, 1962/63

Myriad snowflakes tumble
from a grey fecund sky,
eddying, drifting, falling,
down, down, down
to the inevitable earth.
Fleeting snow patterns
writhe
across the hard ground
and are dispersed
by capricious gusts.
A single flake,
dancing before me,
kisses my cheek,
then falls
to die
on wet flagstones.

B.H.

CHAPTER SIX

LIVERPOOL
NOTEBOOK

My Liverpool student days were over. I had achieved what I had set out to do when I left home and was now entitled to put the letters BA, MCD after my name with the strong possibility of adding AMTPI (Associate Member of the Town Planning Institute) in two years' time. By then I should have had the requisite experience in my chosen profession of Town and Country Planning.

While searching for an appropriate post in Britain or overseas, I found temporary employment in the Planning Department of Kent County Council, which had its office in Maidstone. This was easily reached by rail from St Mary Cray, so it was convenient to live with my parents at this time. It also kept me close to Diane, first while she was temporarily employed at Woodlands Holiday Camp, then when she started her studies at London University.

During that period I received an invitation to fill a temporary teaching vacancy on Merseyside, created when a geography master at a boys' school fell ill and had to stay off work for a month. The headmaster had approached my former Professor of Geography, Robert Steel, at Liverpool, who suggested me as a candidate for the job. This is how I came to spend a few weeks as a teacher in one of the less well-known English public schools (called private schools in the rest of the world – even neighbouring Scotland).

It was easy to return to my old lodgings on Chatham Street and commute to work, but I did not feel very comfortable in my new role. Not regarded as one of the country's top ranked public schools, the place where I taught for a month tried hard to emulate the more elite institutions of its kind, such as Eton and Harrow. Among the great public school traditions that were maintained was an emphasis on sport, especially rugby. Something I was not told when I accepted the temporary job was that the teacher for whom I was substituting was also a sports master. His duties included refereeing school rugby matches, but the game was almost a complete mystery to me.

When, to my great surprise and dismay, and with little notice, I was told that I was expected to referee a game of rugby, I had to admit that I did not know the rules of the sport, that I had never played it and that I had never watched a match. The other masters seemed to find this hard to believe but assured me that all should be well if I studied the book of rules which they gave me. It was called *Why the Whistle Went*. The night before the match, I tried to learn the basic aims and rules of rugby, but failed miserably. I was in a state of near panic when I travelled to work the next morning, and during the day my stomach-churning fear increased as the time for afternoon sports approached. Probably never before had one so entirely ignorant of the game been put in charge of two competing rugby teams, even when they comprised only junior pupils from the same school.

Despite commendable patience and sympathy displayed by the boys, and much advice from knowledgeable young players who tried to explain to me what I should do, the game was a complete shambles. I failed to understand fundamental concepts such as a 'knock on' and was unable to decide what was happening when boys became entangled together in a writhing scrum of bodies, which, as far as I could see, was an essential part of the game. At last I was rescued by one of the schoolmasters who happened to be watching. With a feeling of utmost relief and gratitude, I handed over my responsibilities to him and quickly fled the field.

I achieved greater success in the classroom, even though I did occasionally find myself teaching mathematics, a subject with which I had always had to struggle at school. I was much more comfortable with geography, of course. In one of the classes I took, I gave what I regard as a particularly original lesson in map reading. I was supplied with a set of maps for class use, copies of the Ordnance Survey One Inch to One Mile map of the Snowdon area of North Wales. Being familiar with the region and with the map, I had a little knowledge of the Welsh language, at least of some parts of the vocabulary that relate to places and landforms.

First, I ascertained that no one in the class spoke or understood Welsh. This was particularly necessary because North Wales was not far away. I wrote on the blackboard a list of Welsh words which the boys were asked to translate using the map to determine their meaning. Among the words that I listed on the board were 'afon', 'nant', 'llyn', 'mynydd', 'cwm' and 'coed', meaning 'river', 'stream' 'lake', 'mountain', 'valley' and 'a wood', respectively. The boys seemed to enjoy this novel exercise, which taught them a few words of the Welsh language while testing their skills in map reading.

Among the boys at school was one that, I believe, I never met, whose name I cannot remember, but who remains in my memory because of his being discussed at a staff meeting chaired by the Headmaster. It appears that this senior boy had given offence to the school by refusing to play rugby, preferring football instead. The latter was considered an inferior game, one that was not played at good public schools and thus was unacceptable here. I presume that the errant boy belonged to a local team or club unconnected with his school. With great astonishment, I listened as the schoolmasters, nearly all 'Oxbridge' men, expressed their strong disapproval of the boy whose 'type' was further indicated by his long hair, pointed shoes and the fact that he played drums in one of the local groups!

On hearing this, I shrank in my chair at the back of the staff common room, hoping not to be drawn into the discussion. Fortunately, my views were not sought and I believe that no one at the school was aware of my recent drumming role on the Mersey Scene. I fear that the sports preference of the boy discussed at that meeting might have earned him a reputation which could have coloured references from his school when he applied for university entrance or sought future employment.

I felt much relief when at last it was time to leave the school, although during my short time there I had managed to establish a good relationship with the boys I taught. One junior class even clubbed together to buy me a farewell gift, a record token with a note on which was written, 'To patient & withstanding [*sic*] Mr Hudson, from the undersigned'. Below this were the signatures of the fifteen boys who had contributed. I still have the card and note with the boys' signatures. I stuck them onto the inside sleeve of the LP record that I bought with the gift token augmented from my own pocket. By the time I came to make the purchase, Diane was dead and I felt that Bach might help me endure the pain. I bought a recording of three of his *Sonatas for Violin and Harpsichord* played by Yehudi Menuhin and George Malcolm.

Later, back on Merseyside and now employed as a planning assistant with the Skelmersdale Development Corporation, near Ormskirk, I found myself again in the University precinct, renting a flat directly opposite the Students' Union. It was so close to the University's Victoria Building that the large clock on the redbrick Gothic tower served me well as a timepiece. It could be read easily at a glance, one of the four gilt clock faces, all illuminated at night, filling much of the view from my room and clearly visible from my bed. At about that time I started to keep a notebook from which the following extracts are taken.

November 1963
Jacaranda Club
I heard that The Big Three had broken up after making their first EP 'The Big Three at The Cavern'. This group was itself a product of the break up of an earlier band, Cass and the Cassanovas. I saw their drummer Johnny Hutchinson in the Blue Angel recently. He was with some people from a radio or TV show called *Ready, Steady, Go* and he introduced me as 'one of the brainiest blokes in Liverpool', or something like that. Johnny told me that things were not going well for the group.

10 November 1963
NEMS record shop, Great Charlotte Street
The shop was packed as usual for Saturday. In first place on 'NEMS Top Twenty' list was The Beatles' latest LP, 'With The Beatles'. It was selling amazingly quickly, and I was surprised to see so many older people among the buyers. I watched as an open box full of the records was being rapidly emptied. I bought a Dizzy Gillespie LP of his '45–'46 period and chose to hear one of the big band tracks so that the music had a chance to penetrate the wall of sound coming from neighbouring listening booths.

New Year's Eve 1963
Towards midnight the party was interrupted when everyone rushed outside to greet the New Year. We went to where Belmont Road intersects Breck Road, and there, by the traffic lights, a crowd of people had gathered. We formed circles and sang *Auld Lang Syne* in the roadway. Traffic was halted and some women climbed into a taxi and a bus to kiss the drivers.

January 27, 1964. 8.45pm
Myrtle Street and Chatham Street

> *Soft rain;*
> *Glistening setts;*
> *Uneven, worn,*
> *Wet paving stones*
> *Illuminated by yellow gas-light.*
> *Meagre lights*
> *Multiplied in reflections.*

Late last Saturday night at the Blue Angel, Dave Castle, alto sax player from Alexis Korner's Blues Incorporated, was sitting in with John Rubin's band: wonderful, exciting playing that inspired the resident musicians. He told me that another musician who sometimes played with AK was Art Theman, tenor man with Dave Gelly in the Cambridge University Band I heard at Queen Mary College, London, two years ago. The group was to play at The Cavern on Sunday – 'We won't play like this. Beat stuff for The Cavern crowd!'

(Many years after I wrote this note, I discovered that the performance had been recorded: *Alexis Korner at The Cavern*, recorded 23 February, 1964. Oriole LP [PS40058].)

July 1964
5 Bedford Street North
The Piazza

In front of No. 5, where not long ago could be seen that narrow, deep and black railway cutting which leads to Lime Street Station, there is pleasant paved piazza, recently built over the Liverpool–London mainline. It is overlooked by the Students' Union, the redbrick Gothic Victoria Building and the severely simple white-tiled front of the new engineering block. On the west side is the gabled end of the Catholic *Universe* newspaper building, and beyond rises another of the University's new tower blocks. Just out of sight, hidden by the Students' Union, the huge cone of the new Roman Catholic Cathedral is taking shape. On the east side, separated from the Mathematics block by an unenclosed section of the railway cutting, is a remnant of nineteenth-century Liverpool, a few three-storey slate-roofed brick buildings on the corner of Brownlow Hill and Bedford Street North. There is a general store, a Martin's Bank (University Branch) where The Pack of Cards coffee bar used to be, Parry's University Bookshop, the now empty and bricked-up bookshop of Phillip, Son & Nephew, and No. 5, where I have a first-floor flat. From it I have a distant view of the Liverpool's famous, mythical Liver Birds that top the massive Liver Building, and a bird's-eye view of the piazza. The piazza is like a stage and I can watch what is enacted upon it from my window.

On the nearside of the paved area is a line of concrete bollards, some linked by a metal handrail. Three little children, two girls and a boy, weave in and out between the bollards and under the rail, singing, 'In and out the dusty bluebells'.

A slightly bent old woman, wearing a wine-coloured coat and carrying a laden string shopping bag, is followed by her faithful dog.

She crosses the piazza, then stops to rummage in her bag while the dog gazes up at her. She produces a leash and fastens it to the dog's collar before leading it across busy Brownlow Hill.

Seven small boys on bicycles ride around the piazza, sometimes in a regular circle, sometimes breaking out and interweaving – a boy and bicycle ballet.

Boy and girl sitting on the edge of the piazza by the bollards, talking earnestly.

My Liverpool days were coming to an end. In a couple of months I would be starting a new job in Africa.

Some of the author's drawings. Top: A street scene; bottom: Gothic façade.

*Two of the author's drawings,
featuring female faces.*

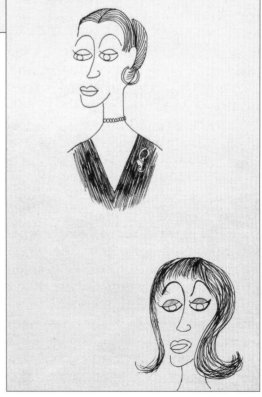

CHAPTER SEVEN

MY PLACE IN THE UNIVERSE

'And when our souls and selves are dissolved away under the metaphysical scrutiny, we continue to be aware of ourselves, of the world around us, to hope, enjoy and suffer, and believe ourselves alive. How fascinating it all is!'
W. Macneile Dixon, *The Human Situation*, 1937

At one time when I was living at Chatham Street, I decided to put on one wall of my room a model of the Solar System, something that would give me a visual image of the Earth in relation to its planetary neighbours and the Sun, and to the vast space between. I marked the positions of the Sun and the nine planets with labelled white paper arrows, which showed up clearly against the patterned wallpaper. I was aware that what I represented on the wall of my room was but a minute portion of the Universe.

The simple model on the wall helped me keep a sense of proportion in my life. When problems on my mind seemed overwhelming, contemplation of the speck that was Earth spinning in the vastness of space made any difficulties I might be experiencing or any concerns of mine seem negligible. Conversely, on occasions when I might have felt an inflated sense of self-importance, the thought that I was but a minute entity on an insignificant planet put my position in the order of things into a humbling perspective.

Contemplation of space and time, of existence and of my experience of all this filled me with a sense of wonder. I marvelled at the universe and, for the most part, I was glad that I was here to enjoy it. There were times, however, when my consciousness of the imperfect world and despair at the folly of humanity aroused in me a feeling of angst.

One day, as I walked through downtown Liverpool where the streets were thronged with people hurrying about their business, I imagined a gigantic boot coming down and crushing them all like ants. I quickly realised that I was one of those people in the streets, a member of this mass of humanity, each individual being a person like me with feelings, hopes and concerns, and my sympathy for these fellow creatures soon returned.

It was mainly after my five years as a university student that I began to read works of philosophy and science. I was aware that people like me, who had studied arts or humanities subjects, were generally ignorant on scientific matters, while those trained in science and related fields, such as medicine and engineering, were often widely read in literature and accomplished in some of the arts.

In Liverpool University's jazz fraternity – a mainly male society – students from science, engineering and medicine were prominent among the leading musicians. I must have learned something in my lower school chemistry, physics and biology lessons but it was not until I began to read popular science books by authors such as Jacob Bronowski, Banesh Hoffmann, Fred Hoyle and Anthony Barnett that I

The author on board the New Brighton Ferry, c. 1961, in his student days.

started to appreciate the excitement of scientific research and discovery as well as the amazing nature of the universe. I am indebted to writers such as these, eminent scientists who had the ability and willingness to communicate to ordinary people some of the basic problems and concepts of their fields and the deep satisfaction they gained in their search for answers to fundamental questions.

In 1960 I attended a lecture given by one of these great science communicators, Hermann Bondi. He spoke about the expanding universe and the evidence for this provided by the Doppler Effect on starlight and the resultant red shift. This wonderful opportunity arose when, at the suggestion of Allan Patmore, one of my geography lecturers at Liverpool, I applied for and was awarded an exhibition, which enabled me to attend the Annual Conference of the British Association for the Advancement of Science, held that year in Cardiff.

For me, Professor Bondi's lecture was one of the highlights of the meeting. The conference also enabled me to see and hear some distinguished geographers of the day, both in the lecture hall and in the field on trips into the valleys and along the coast of South Wales. There, in real life, were L. Dudley Stamp and S.W. Wooldridge, writers of all those textbooks! A memorable part of this Welsh experience was a concert in which performances were given by the celebrated Treorchy Male Voice Choir and by the harpist, Ossian Ellis, who demonstrated the art of penillion singing.

I found things in science that seemed as far removed from the world of reality as any tale of the supernatural, whether in myth or legend or in any of the great books of established religion. *The Strange Story of the Quantum*, to use the title of Hoffmann's book, was, for me, not only an extraordinary trail of human discovery, but a revelation of a subatomic world in which the seemingly impossible is normal. What won my respect for science – while my attitude towards religion became increasingly dismissive – was its passion for exploration, its rigorous pursuit of knowledge and truth and its built-in system of self-scrutiny. It fed the great human demand for knowledge about the universe, and everyone was invited to prove its findings wrong.

This seemed an excellent way to get nearer to the truth of the matter. There are other ways. Like most book lovers, I read fiction mainly for the pleasure that novels and short stories give with their intriguing tales, fascinating characters and delightful evocations of places and times. Gradually, however, I began to realise that these creative works contributed to our understanding of the world and, in particular, of the human condition. Other artistic endeavours, such as painting and music, no doubt make similar contributions to our understanding but to me it is less clear how this is achieved. It is possible that created forms in sound or paint can help us to be receptive to understanding of a kind different from that gained from what we call rational thought processes.

For some reason, a quotation from the Bible comes to mind here: 'Be still, and know that I am God' (Psalms 46:10). Perhaps I am opposed less to religion than to bigoted holders of religious beliefs. It is those who are certain that they are in possession of the absolute truth that create most of the world's troubles and pose the greatest threat to humanity.

One of my religious friends whom I did not regard as a threat of any kind was the student who lodged with me in Huyton when we were both freshers at Liverpool. He was a Christian, either a new convert or one whose faith had been renewed because of some recent experience. We shared a room in the semi-detached suburban house, and when, the first night of our residence there, we were retiring to our respective beds, he raised the matter of his faith and religious practices. In particular, he asked if it would bother me if he knelt and said his prayers before going to bed. I told him that, while I did not share his beliefs, I had no objection to his praying in my presence.

My roommate seemed relieved to be able to talk with me freely about some recent unhappy experiences in his life and the religious faith that gave him strength to face his problems. When an itinerant evangelist came to the University, my Christian friend persuaded me to hear the man give a talk on 'The Impossibility of Agnosticism' and to meet the speaker afterwards. The evangelist's talk and the discussion I had with the speaker did not change my views.

Between that time and the completion of my university studies at Liverpool, I found little time for reading and thinking much about anything but my coursework and jazz. Once, in response to a brief pang of intellectual guilt as I passed a temporary bookstall in the Students' Union, I bought a copy of *Existentialism, Marxism and Anarchism* by Herbert Read. Later, I read this brief work with interest, but reading of this kind was very rare until I had completed my formal studies at Liverpool.

As I wrote the previous couple of sentences, my thoughts went off at a tangent, as they are wont to do. Consider this: While at Reading, my serious reading included works by Herbert Read whom I read avidly. English is a very funny written and spoken language! The odd quirks of spelling and pronunciation in English have tempted me to write limericks that celebrate this quality. Here is one inspired by a direction sign I saw while travelling by bus along the M1 motorway north-west of London.

There was a young lady from Dunstable
Who had an affair with a constable,
But she never would cease
Chasing other police,
So the relationship grew very unstable.

Later, I penned the following:

An Irishman in Cheadle Hulme
Spun flax and wove it on a loom.
While he carded and combed
One night he was bombed.
His remains were interred in a tomb.

Much as I enjoyed English at school, I chose Geography as my principal subject of study at university. This was mainly because of my interest in place and landscape. It was also a suitable preparation for a course and career in Town and Country Planning, a profession I saw as one contributing to the wise use of the world's resources and the protection of its beauty

At Bromley Grammar School, Kent, where I received my secondary education, I had to choose between History and Geography at Advanced Level, although I would have preferred to have taken both. Unfortunately for me, the school timetable did not allow this combination. This was especially disappointing because I was conscious of the importance of geographical factors in the history of humanity and of the role of history in the evolution of the humanised landscape and in the development of spatial patterns of human activity. The two subjects are complementary in that they treat the human experience on earth in the context of time and space.

My interest in the world's development over time was not limited to the relatively recent period since the emergence of humankind. Geological and geomorphological processes over aeons fascinated me, particularly the way that these left their mark on the present landscape and influenced human life today.

My teenage bicycle tours round England made me acutely aware of the grain of the physical landscape, particularly the asymmetrical ridges which resulted from the erosion of the gently folded rocks of the south-east and the dissected uplands and glaciated highlands of the north. As my university and later studies increased my knowledge of geomorphology, I began to gain a deeper understanding of the familiar Cleveland landscape around Hobdale, the place where I was born and spent much of my childhood. It came as a revelation to discover that the flat-bottomed valley in which stood the first school I attended as an infant was a lake at the end of the last Ice Age. The rich black soil of the old lake floor was used for allotment gardens, and there were still marshy patches that contained shallow ponds. Here I used to collect frogspawn and tadpoles.

It was my experience of landscape and love of place that stimulated my interest in geography; that and my fascination with strange lands and people. My delight in music and pleasure in performing on stage might have directed me towards a career as an entertainer of some kind, but my passion for the earth and the dramas enacted upon it took precedence in my choice of work and lifestyle. Eventually, I found myself enjoying performing to audiences of students, my stage the rostrum, the lecture theatre my regular venue. In this way I found a satisfying outlet for my creative urge and my need to communicate.

CHAPTER EIGHT

THE GLOBE ENCIRCLED, A TRIANGLE COMPLETED

'The trade was triangular. Liverpool shipped a cargo of
Lancashire cottons to West Africa, exchanged it for slaves, took
the slaves to the West Indies, and there turned them into a
cargo of cotton, sugar and tobacco for Britain.'
Eric Williams, ' The Golden Age of the Slave System in Britain',
Journal of Negro History, 25, 1940

When I left university, I entered the planning profession I had chosen as a grammar school boy and had studied for at Liverpool. Liverpool University had a long, established reputation for both geography and town planning. The idea of pursuing an academic career also crossed my mind for, on gaining my bachelor's degree, I had been invited to do research in the Geography Department. I decided to stick to my original plan and study for Liverpool's Master of Civic Design degree, one recognised by the Town Planning Institute. In this way I would achieve both a master's degree and a professional qualification as a town and country planner. With the support of Robert Steel, the John Rankin Professor of Geography, I obtained a Liverpool University Scholarship and remained a student there for two more years before joining the staff of the Skelmersdale Development Corporation in a former coal mining community just north of Liverpool. While there, I was involved in the early stages of planning Skelmersdale New Town.

Now deprived of both Diane and my life in university jazz, I became determined to go overseas and see the world. In this I was assisted by some of the academic staff of the Geography Department. Andrew Learmonth tried to find me work at an Indian research centre with which he was associated. In a letter of recommendation dated 12 July 1962, he wrote, 'He is one of the best four or five geographers we have produced in as many years and, though he missed his first, this was perhaps due to a wholly venial interest in some of the less academic activities of the University.' Jazz, it seems, had deprived me of a first class degree at Liverpool.

It was Professor Robert Steel who recommended me for a lecturing post he had heard about at a new university in the recently independent West African country of Ghana, formerly the Gold Coast. By that time I had already applied for a Commonwealth Scholarship to the University of Hong Kong, something I had seen advertised in a national newspaper. Hong Kong appealed strongly because it was very far away, on the other side of the world in fact; and it was on the doorstep of China, a country that held a particular fascination for me because of its ancient culture and its revolutionary transformation. I also had a preference to do research because I felt insufficiently experienced as a planner or prepared as an academic to teach geography and planning at university level. Moreover, I wanted a change of focus from Africa, which loomed large among Liverpool's Geography Department teaching and research interests. At that time the 'Mysterious Orient' appealed to me more strongly than the 'Dark Continent', even though I was excited by the optimistic prospects of the newly independent African countries. For me, *Go Ghana*, an exuberant tune composed by Scottish jazz clarinettist Sandy Brown, expressed the international political mood of the period.

After interviews in London, I received a firm offer of a job in Ghana, but there was a long delay in the announcement of the Hong Kong scholarship. With the outcome of my scholarship application in doubt, I decided to accept the offer of a lecturing post at Kwame Nkrumah University of Science and Technology (KNUST), Kumasi. Soon after I agreed to join KNUST, I received the much desired scholarship offer. Annoyed at the timing of events, I nevertheless decided against letting down the African university and, risking losing my chance to go to Hong Kong, I requested a deferral of the Commonwealth Scholarship. Technically, I was required to reapply, but as things turned out, I was able to spend one academic year teaching in Ghana before starting my PhD research at the University of Hong Kong. The year's delay changed the course of my life utterly. It was in September 1965, when I eventually flew to Hong Kong, that the Jamaican woman who was to become my wife also arrived there. That is another story.

Ghana is in a part of Africa that for centuries had strong commercial links with Liverpool. Among the physical reminders of Liverpool's historical connection with West Africa were the Goree Piazzas, two massive warehouses which formerly stood by the docks. These old buildings were named after one of the main slave trading centres, Gorée Island, off Senegal. Damaged by Hitler's bombs during the Blitz, the Goree Piazzas were finally demolished in 1958. The slave trade, the export of manufactured goods and the import of cotton, sugar and other produce of Empire made Liverpool a great port city in the eighteenth and nineteenth centuries. I was well aware of this when I went to Ghana and felt especially sensitive to the tragic memories of slavery stored in the walls of the grim European castles at Elmina, Axim and Prince's Town when I visited them. Little could I have imagined then that I would eventually marry a woman whose African ancestors almost certainly came from that part of the world, some possibly passing through those very fortresses from which I gazed out to sea, imagining the slave ships anchored offshore. Many of those were Liverpool vessels and after taking on their human cargo, they sailed from Africa to the Americas, a long and often hazardous voyage across the Atlantic. Millions of Africans were transported from their homelands in this cruel trade,

The seventeenth-century Brandenburger Fort at Princes Town, Ghana.

Cape Coast Castle, Ghana: a former British slave trading centre.

many thousands dying in the overcrowded squalid conditions below deck, others destined to suffer and die in the plantations where they were forced to work when sold into slavery. That is how black people came to America. Many were taken to the islands of the Caribbean, and from there ships sailed back to England with cargoes of sugar, rum, cotton and tobacco bound for London, Bristol and Liverpool.

This pattern of commerce came to be known by historians as the Triangular Trade, its three corners being in Europe, Africa and America. Close to the old Liverpool docks is Jamaica Street, another reminder of the city's involvement in this trade. Jamaica was the source of much of Britain's slave-generated wealth in the eighteenth century and it was in that Caribbean country that I married Anne. The ceremony was held at the University Chapel on the site of a former sugar estate which had been worked by African slaves in years gone by. The handsome building in which we exchanged our wedding vows was originally a curing house on another sugar estate across the island. In 1956 it had been transferred, stone by stone, from its original site to the Mona campus of the University of the West Indies. It bears the date of its original construction, 1799, carved into the stonework.

When I travelled to Jamaica, I completed the triangle, the old trade route from Liverpool to West Africa and thence to the West Indies. On my return to England with my wife, I had also completed my first journey round the globe. After my year in Ghana, I returned to England before travelling via Moscow, Bombay, Madras, Singapore and Bangkok to Hong Kong. From Hong Kong I eventually returned to England, crossing the Pacific and spending time in Canada and Jamaica on the way.

A montage of Liverpool newspaper and other cuttings in the author's MacDonnell Road flat, Hong Kong.

On my fateful flight from Hong Kong to Jamaica, I broke my journey in Toronto. There I caught up with a couple of my old Liverpool friends, Terry, a girl who used to work at the Jacaranda, and her husband, a student contemporary of mine, then engaged in research at the University of Toronto. I arranged to meet Terry at her new workplace, a coffee bar in Yorkville, at that time Toronto's hippy quarter. While we were chatting, a crowd of young people came in whose dress and behaviour seemed ostentatiously bohemian. One of them was carrying a pair of legs from a tailor's dummy. Glancing at the hippies, then turning to me, Terry said in her broad Liverpool accent, 'You know, Brian, we've seen all dis before, 'aven't we?'

During my two years in Hong Kong, I continued to feel the presence of Liverpool. The music of The Beatles, Gerry and the Pacemakers, The

Dunns River Beach, Jamaica: a family holiday photograph.

Searchers and other Merseyside groups could be heard everywhere. Many of the vessels that anchored in the great harbour were Liverpool ships. The professor of architecture who supervised my PhD thesis was a Liverpool graduate and the warden of Hong Kong University's Eliot Hall, where I lived for a while, had previously worked in the Veterinary Science Department of Liverpool University. By now, my former Liverpool girlfriend, Helen, had left Singapore and was teaching in a British school in Hong Kong and, with her help, I organised a Scouse party which was held in my Eliot Hall flat. Scouse, the famous Liverpool dish, prepared by Chinese cooks under Helen's supervision, was served to my party guests, among whom was my future wife.

It was at the University of Hong Kong that I met Anne, the Jamaican graduate student with whom I fell in love. When she returned to her

Arthur Dooley's bronze soldier on the author's balcony in Brisbane.

home in Kingston, I followed her, intent on making her my wife. Shortly after our marriage, I took Anne back to England, travelling by sea across the Atlantic. Calling at ports in Colombia, Venezuela, the Canary Islands and northern Spain along the way, our Spanish ship eventually reached England, docking in Southampton. I had now travelled all the way round the world, albeit without ever crossing the Equator. I accomplished that feat at a later date, on a trip from Jamaica to Peru, again in the company of Anne, with whom I had returned to the Caribbean with our infant son after spending two years in England. During that time we visited my old Liverpool haunts. By then, most of my Liverpool student and musician friends had scattered, but Geography classmate and jazz trumpeter Phil Morris came from out of town with his wife to meet Anne and me in Ye Cracke. We still keep in touch, and like many of my Liverpool University jazz musician contemporaries, he still plays regularly. Now his gigs are held in Australia as he lives on a mountaintop in northern New South Wales, not far from where Anne and I have our flat in the middle of Brisbane, just over the border in Queensland. Phil is the 'Dante' in the story that follows.

CHAPTER NINE

P.S.

THE BEATLES AND ME

'P.S. So you can't remember playing with The Beatles?
I remember you saying that you once played a gig where
The Beatles were the interval band . . . And one of my cocktail
party boasts has always been "I used to play guitar in Liverpool
with a drummer who once played a gig where The Beatles
were the interval band . . ." So must I now drop this from my
elderly pick-up lines??? Think HARD, Brian . . .'

Professor Emeritus Fergus Craik,
formerly Head of the Department of Psychology,
University of Toronto, Canada, and world authority on ageing and
memory. From an e-mail message dated 11 May 2006

I may have said that, and it may well be true – but I can't remember. After all, it all happened half a century ago. Once, during my student days, I visited the Liverpool College of Art, which boasts John Lennon and Stuart Sutcliffe among its former students. Unknown to me and the rest of the world then, those young men were soon to become famous as members of The Beatles, a group that was still in its embryonic stage the day I went to the art college.

I was accompanying a university friend of mine who hoped to see a girl, an art student, with whom he had fallen in love. Like Dante who worshipped his beloved Beatrice from afar, my companion had not made his feelings known to the object of his passion. Indeed, my lovelorn friend seemed to think that he could have no hope of having his affection returned by one so beautiful. Nevertheless, at my urging, we went to the college where this Liverpool Beatrice was a student, if only to feast our eyes on her beauty. As things turned out, we did not even catch a distant glimpse of her.

During our wanderings in the art college, we passed a hall with a stage on which three or four black-clad youths were dismantling and removing their musical equipment, including amplifiers and drums. I can hear in my imagination my companion telling me, 'They're The Beatles'. He may have said, 'Silver Beetles', the group's earlier name. I am not sure that I had heard of them before, but my student friend was also a local jazz musician and probably knew better than I the Merseyside music scene.

On reflection, there was something very beetle-like about the youths in their tight fitting black clothes as they busied themselves on and off the stage. By that time, John Lennon and Stuart Sutcliffe may have no longer been students at the college, but perhaps they played gigs there or used the hall for practice. It is possible that the group we saw at the art college that day was The Quarrymen, in which Lennon and Sutcliffe played before The Beatles emerged. One former Rhythm Club member recalls a University band practice held in the art college where we saw John Lennon giving guitar instruction to Paul McCartney, or vice versa, but I have no recollection of this.

Many years after our student days, the Dante of my story wrote me a letter recalling a gig at which a Liverpool University jazz band and The Beatles were playing. Another of my fellow university jazz musicians has no doubts that our band shared at least one gig with The Beatles and that we all repaired to a nearby pub while the despised beat group was on stage. I may well have been there with The Beatles, but, having played at several events where local rock groups were also on the programme, it is probable that I took no particular notice of a band which, unknown to us then, was soon to achieve unparalleled fame in the world of popular music.

It was largely through the efforts of Brian Epstein that The Beatles achieved their amazing success and, by strange coincidence, the paths of those remarkable Liverpudlians crossed mine on Thursday, 9 November 1961. On that day, according to the well-known story, Epstein, having become aware of the group's local popularity, dropped into The Cavern and spoke with The Beatles in the band room. Their conversation that afternoon eventually led to a business association that achieved fame and fortune for them all. I was also in The Cavern that day, but the consequences of my visit were less spectacular.

By this time, the former jazz club on Mathew Street had become mainly a venue for rock music, but it still put on occasional jazz performances. On that November night, American tenorman Zoot Sims was playing with a top British group, including Ronnie Scott, sufficient reason for my presence in The Cavern audience. The Beatles were not known to be jazz lovers, so I think it unlikely that they were still around that evening when I was enjoying my kind of music in the exciting atmosphere of Liverpool's famous cellar club.

I may have encountered The Beatles at another Liverpool club, the Jacaranda, a onetime haunt of theirs. A girlfriend of Ringo Starr worked there as a waitress, a vivacious blonde from whose hands I received many a frothy coffee. Ringo's former bandleader, Rory Storm, was also a frequent Jacaranda customer, and I used to marvel that one who stuttered so badly when speaking experienced no problem when singing onstage.

I also used to go to the Blue Angel, another club frequented by The Beatles and it was there that I met Paul McCartney's brother, Michael. At that time, under the assumed name of Mike McGear, he was a member of the satirical Liverpool group, Scaffold.

Soon after The Beatles first achieved international fame, I found myself in very close proximity to them. It was in a suburban Liverpool street. They were in a limousine coming from Speke, now Liverpool John Lennon Airport. I was returning home, travelling in the same direction on the top deck of a bus. As my bus followed its route through the streets, I wondered why so many people were lining the kerb as we drove past. The reason for the crowds became apparent as the traffic, including my bus, was stopped to allow a long black motorcar to pass unimpeded down the street towards the city centre. I then realised that it must be The Beatles returning in triumph to Liverpool, where they were to be honoured with a civic reception.

Peering down from my window seat on top of the stationary bus, I saw little more than the roof of the vehicle in which the now famous rock group was travelling. I caught a glimpse of a hand (or was it a nose, Ringo's perhaps?) poking from a nearside passenger window, but that was all.

All, that is, as far as my involvement in the world of The Beatles went. Their music, however, continued to be part of my life, often providing a leitmotif to the drama of human experience I shared on the world stage. Issued shortly before I left England with my wife Anne and infant son Dominic to return to Jamaica, *Hey Jude* reflected aspects of my life up to that time. Having found her, I had, as the song advises, let her under my skin and gone out to get her.

The author and his wife in a studio portrait, Australia, 1990.

Other Liverpool titles from The History Press

Memories of John Lennon
Introduced and Edited by Yoko Ono
978-0-7509-4384-0

The Story of Liverpool
Alex Tulloch
978-0-7509-4508-0

For What It's Worth: My Liverpool Childhood
Bryan Kelly
978-0-7509-4155-6

Aintree Days
Alex Tulloch
978-0-7509-4318-5